"Bob Erdmann provide⸱ ⸱⸱⸱der-standing of the historic theology of work and tl⸱ This thought-provoking book wiⅡ c⸱⸱⸱

Dr. Jⅇ ⸱⸱⸱ i
Author, speaker, city director for
Campus Crusade for Christ in the Cleveland/NEO area

"I have known, observed, and appreciated Bob Erdmann for over three decades. What he says and how he lives align beautifully. He's now given us a wonderful gift—a clear, concise, and well thought-out 'handbook' on the biblical underpinnings and history of work. I trust it will help you as it's helped me!"

John D. Beckett
Chairman, The Beckett Companies
Author, *Loving Monday* and *Mastering Monday*

"Bob Erdmann has captured the concept of work from creation through today and into the future. The reader can grasp work from God's perspective; see how various cultures remolded it; and how the church of today can redeem it.
"As an educator, I walked away with the understanding that each of us has been given a 'garden' to care for and we should invest our energy in 'tending that garden.' For me, that garden was the classroom, the school, the district, and ultimately the field of education in America."

Finn Laursen
Executive director,
Christian Educators Association International

"Even before this book hit the printing press, I have been recommending it to college students and those already in the workforce. I have 20 years' experience in the secular workplace and am currently in my 18th year as a full-time missionary. I have been inspired and encouraged, and my perspective on work in the secular workplace has been challenged and changed for the better. If the principles in this book were embraced by all Christ-followers, His light would shine much brighter and His kingdom would be advanced significantly."

Chaplain Bill Goodrich
God Cares Ministry

The Call to Work
(A Biblical Perspective)

by

ROBERT H. ERDMANN

The Call to Work
(A Biblical Perspective)
Copyright 2012 by Robert H. Erdmann

All rights reserved. Published by Brownstone Books Division, LMS
Products, Inc., P. O. Box 40511, Cleveland, OH (440) 667-3736.

ISBN: 978-0-9855044-0-3

First Edition
Library of Congress Catalog No. 2012938832
Unless indicated otherwise, Scripture quotations are taken from
the New American Standard Bible, Copyright 1960, 1962, 1963, 1968,
1971, 1972, 1973, 1975, 1977, 1995 by The Lockman Foundation.
Used by permission. (www.Lockman.org)

Please visit the author's website at www.brownstonebooks.org

Contents

Preface

"If man's fulfillment of his nature is to be found in the full
expression of his divine creativeness, then we urgently need a
Christian doctrine of work, which shall provide not only for
proper conditions of employment, but also that the work shall
be such as a man may do with his whole heart, and that he
shall do it for the very work's sake."

Dorothy Sayers

T HERE ARE MANY GOOD BOOKS ON what has come to be known as
marketplace ministry, i.e., how to serve God in your workplace.
Topics include how to witness, how to better serve your boss and/
or your employer, how to be that wise man or woman of God who
never rattles and always has a kind word, who exercises their gift of
leadership in a God-pleasing way, and who creates a better overall
environment around them.

This book is not about marketplace ministry. Very simply, this
book explores the place secular work itself has in God's plan for you.
This topic comes before the previous paragraph, which describes the
things you would be doing anyway as a person of God. No, this is
an exploration of what and how God thinks about work at the fun-
damental level. That's why we start in Genesis to uncover a reason
why we work in the first place. It therefore becomes a book on the
theology of work.

Very few things are more important for our attitude about life and what to do with it than work itself. This is especially true if you are concerned about what God may think about your work and activities in the secular realm. I assure you, this discussion will not be dull if you take seriously the purpose in life for which God created you! I will do my best to make it as readable as possible for the skeptic as well as the Kingdom minded.

Maybe you have questions like, "Why do I feel so unfulfilled in my work?" or "Why does Friday seem so far off?" or "Why does the church speak so sparingly about secular work?" or "Why am I so overworked and underpaid?" or "Does God care about what I'm doing from 9 to 5?" or "How can I serve God full time?" Those are all questions I had that prompted this study, and for which I found unanticipated answers. The answers filled a hole of understanding for me, and will for you, too. It was as if these thoughts were hidden in plain sight, as they say. You can judge for yourself as we go along.

For over two millennia now, much rhetoric has been spoken and much ink spilled on the subject of work: what it is and how you do it. Approaching it from a secular viewpoint, I have come to see, will never come to solid ground. Phrases like, "as many definitions as there are people" or "defining work is a messy business" or "it depends on the culture" belie a not-so-hidden exasperation of nailing down what exactly we're dealing with. The mere fact that so many have tried, however, speaks volumes to me of just how important this subject is in the lives of mankind. Most of the time we are left with a "can't live with it, can't live without it" mentality that doesn't solve anything.

Down deep, we really do want to be productive, but there is something down in our souls that rebels at having to do it, especially in less than perfect circumstances. So where is the disconnect? Did something happen in history that marred the human psyche so that we are repelled by having to do something we are amazingly well equipped by God to do, namely aggressive, productive work?

Secular historians usually start with the Greeks in about 500 BC as the stage at which Plato and Aristotle spoke on the subject with very different conclusions than many of us would now. This we will explore in some detail later.

But for Judeo/Christian peoples, what about the Bible that goes back to our beginning? Surely this book has something to say on a subject so prominent in the lives of us all. If that is so, where is the exposition of it? What is there for those of us who hunger for a firm foundation on which to build that major part of our lives—that fulfills our longings to be productive and useful, but also provides financially for our families and the work of God on earth?

Where, I say, is that explanation that lays out His will and purpose for us? Is the Bible silent on this subject? And what about the pastor or priest who is not quite able to recommend a secular profession to someone who wants to serve God full time? I maintain that God does, in fact, speak loudly about this subject if we have ears to hear, the exposition of which is the core purpose of this book.

It was not until the middle of the twentieth century that much scholarly work of consequence was done from within the church on the question of work. In particular, the question remains why the church has not been able to elevate secular–commercial vocations beyond their second-tier relationship to the sacred, a place assigned to it as far back as the Greek philosophers. This work has included the thoughts of people like Dorothy Sayers, Larry Peabody, Lee Hardy, John Beckett, Christian Smith, Nancy Pearcy, Paul Stevens, and others—and the Christian media typified by Andree Seu and Marvin Olasky. There is no point in repeating their very thoughtful and useful work. I will, however, be quoting them liberally herein.

What I have not noticed, however, is a simple articulation of the biblical roots of the theology of work itself. This had been hidden to me and I dare say to many others, even though it has been pointed out by some that there is still a dichotomy between the sacred and secular realms of activity. Pretty obvious, really, but what has God said about it from the beginning? What is the biblical grounding for our assertions that there is a level playing field that we are all on, with no Kingdom hierarchy anywhere? What is the biblical grounding for asserting that work is good and that we should all be hard at it? Also, are there common calls to which we must all answer? The answer to that of course is yes, but what are they?

In recent years, as I have pondered my own gifting in engineering and sales activities, there were some thoughts from others hanging over me about why I wasn't serving the Lord "full time" as a pastor. I then had to ask myself, is God pleased with or does He even care about what I *am* doing full time, namely, the manufacture and sale of parts for locomotives and freight cars? (You can insert your own firmly secular–commercial activities here).

It was and is important to me to know however, that He *does* know and *is* happy about what I am doing and pleased that I am doing it! Not only that, I discerned that if I don't exercise this gift and vocation, or succumb to the subtle suggestion that a gift isn't really worth much spiritually because it's "only a job," a contribution to the Society of Man is missing.

To put it another way, if I do know God has equipped me with certain talents but I let them languish, or let someone talk me out of them, or just plain ignore them, I am in danger of being the last man in the parable of the talents.[1] This is the one whom the Lord described as "wicked and lazy" for hiding his talent rather than investing (using) it and then proclaimed the "worthless slave (should be cast) into the outer darkness." That is a person we don't want to be and it's not a place we want to be.

Our narrative starts, then, at the very beginning of time at Creation. God had a plan to have certain creatures, namely us, endowed with the ability to fellowship with Him and to partner with Him in the ongoing creation of whatever might come out of His mind as well as ours. The wording in Genesis is shot through with His inclusion of man to work with, create in, and have dominion over the Creation He had just finished.

As if to emphasize the superior role man had in the created order, God began by assigning Adam the intellectual task of giving names to all the other creatures. This is not a fellowship of equals of man and the animals, as naturalists would have us believe. This is fellowship of God with man at a level the animals could not attain to. We will examine this wondrous state in more detail later; however, we all know it didn't last.

---

1. Matt. 25:14–30.

As the relationship of man with God continued to deteriorate after the Fall, the human race suffered a near extinction at the Flood, but it continued an apostate existence through the rebellion at Babel and the rise of humanistic and mystical religions that came out of man's mind, including pagan rites, Eastern mysticism, and humanistic philosophies such as what is now known as Greek Dualism. This carried on right to the time of Christ and beyond.

The redemptive work of Christ on the Cross changed everything for everyone, but sometimes overlooked is His complete demolishing of the social stratification that had come out of the mind of man in every society on earth. However, man's ideas and philosophies eventually overwhelmed even the Church on earth and hit the ground running just a couple centuries after Christ.

Just how deeply this sacred/secular way of thinking invaded the church is illustrated by the state of the Church in the Middle Ages. They are also called the "Dark" Ages for a reason. This period of time represents the most ignoble efforts of man to separate the ecclesiastical structure of the church from the common person. Man put in place elaborate structures and doctrines that resulted in the subjugation of the masses to the interpretations and declarations of a few, who declared that the real way to God is interrupted by the active life, which included acts of service to others! Instead, they said we just needed to quiet our spirit and contemplate God. A refusal to subject oneself to this church structure or to search the Scriptures on one's own often resulted in torture and execution by the church itself!

Does this all sound like too harsh an indictment of the church? Check it out for yourself.[2]

It took a major wrenching around of the way man perceives God in the changes wrought by the Reformation. This had the promise of setting all men free to come to God directly, rather than through an intermediary priest, and to serve Him again in the way they had

---

2. William Byron Forbush (ed.), *Fox's Book of Martyrs*, Grand Rapids, MI, Zondervan, 1968, and John S. Oyer and Robert S. Krieder, *Mirror of the Martyrs*, Intercourse, PA, Good Books, 1990. These two books describe the persecution by the orthodox church of confessing believers, "*Fox's*" incidents being both before and after the Reformation, and "*Mirrors*" contains incidents after.

been created through their gifting and vocations, a subject on which the reformers had a lot to say.

Much of that did take place; however, the church remains mired in a structure that guarantees the special role played by certain people who graduate from specific schools called "seminaries," while the masses of the faithful struggle to believe they are doing anything special for God except from within the church, as we respond to a liturgy once a week and spend a couple of evenings a week in committee meetings, helping to propagate the institution. None of this helps "lay" people along the vocational path God has called *them* to.

Although there are always exceptions to these observations, it is my perception, based on several decades in the church, that a second Reformation is needed and may be on the horizon. I believe—along with the rising voices of many others—that the fellowship God originally allowed Himself with man in the Garden, along with the equipping and creative opportunities He gave to man, is not present or possible the way our thinking, especially Western Greek–thinking churches, is structured.

The call of the Church is to proclaim the Word, which it does quite well, and equip the saints, which it does quite badly. This treatise is about equipping the saints, and why it requires a reexamination of the way the current church thinks and is structured. We will, therefore, trace the theme of work throughout history, beginning at the Creation, through post-Flood, worldly philosophers, the time of Christ, the Dark Ages, the Reformation, and our current day, with a glance into the future. It's an enlightening trip!

And one more thing: You will probably notice several areas and subjects where an elaboration of thought would have been possible. I, in fact, had to resist the temptation to do so in many places, because there is a deliberate, focused thread in this piece about work and its fate through the ages. I have used many thoughtful sources in my discovery of this thread. The Suggested Reading list at the end will provide much fodder for those disposed to pursue the matter further and follow any delightful rabbit trail. My own search will not end when this treatise ends.

Part One
The History of Work

Chapter One
The Creation of Work

" . . . and there was no man to cultivate the ground."

Gen. 2:5

CREATIVE WORK IS A RECURRING THEME from the very beginning of what God did in the Creation. His description of His own activities, the creative opportunities He gave to Adam, the curse after the Fall, the occupations of the people, and the rescue of civilization itself is *centered on the status of work*. Productive work was a major part of what He had in mind for all of us from the very beginning.

The Fall interrupted that plan by imposing stiff penalties on our ability to do work. However, the redemptive work of Jesus Christ and the regenerative work of the Holy Spirit afforded us the opportunity to continue in the way that God had planned from the beginning. Seeing things in this way gives us a better understanding of an oft-quoted passage: "For we are His workmanship, created in Christ Jesus for good works, which God prepared beforehand that we should walk in them."[3] But we are ahead of ourselves. Let's

---

3. Eph. 2:10.

expand these thoughts, taking them one at a time, to see the central place our gifting and, yes, calling to work have had in the economy of God.

THE CREATION

The majestic, overwhelming, sublime, supernatural act of Creation is described in the Bible with the very pedantic word, *work*.

> *"And by the seventh day God completed His work which He had done; and He rested on the seventh day from all His work which He had done."* Gen. 2:2

Other, more colorful terms come to mind to describe God's activities at the time of Creation: words such as *danced, sang, laughed, shouted,* or *clapped*. Maybe He did all those things and more, but He says only of Himself that He worked. God had a purpose in choosing His phraseology for, as we shall see, after the Creation there begins a continuous thread of work as the unfolding of the Society of Man takes place, in fact, before we even existed.

THE CREATION AND CALL OF ADAM

Here, then, is the very tight sequence of the narrative describing the creation of man and his placement into the created order of the earth. An announcement of what is about to be described is even made beginning in Genesis to begin the narrative of man.

> *"This is the account of the heavens and the earth when they were created, in the day that the Lord God made earth and heaven."* Gen. 2:4

> *"Now no shrub of the field was yet in the earth, and no plant of the field had yet sprouted, for the Lord God had not sent rain upon the earth;* and there was no man to cultivate the ground." Gen. 2:5

The Lord made this observation about work *before* there was any man on the earth. Why would He do this unless it was part of His master plan that the continuation of His own creative work was and is *a part* of our reason to exist!

> *"But a mist used to rise from the earth and water the whole surface of the ground. Then the Lord God formed man of dust from the ground, and breathed into his nostrils the breath of life; and man became a living being."* Gen. 2:6, 7

Man does now exist with the very breath of God in his nostrils. God did not bring any other creature into being in this way. I believe God's breath imparted to us a portion of His essence, that being, among other things, the ability to bring into existence ideas and things that weren't there before.

> *"The Lord God planted a garden toward the east, in Eden; and there He placed the man whom He had formed."* Gen. 2:8

Immediately after his creation, man is put in his place of perfect abode to be with and commune with God: the Garden in Eden.

> *"And out of the ground the Lord God caused to grow every tree that is pleasing to the sight and good for food; the tree of life also in the midst of the garden, and the tree of the knowledge of good and evil. Now a river flowed out of Eden to water the garden; and from there it divided and became four rivers. The name of the first is Pishon; it flows around the whole land of Havilah, where there is gold. And the gold of that land is good; the bdellium and the onyx stone are there. And the name of the second river is Gihon; it flows around the whole land of Cush. And the name of the third river is Tigris; it flows east of Assyria. And the fourth river is the Euphrates."* Gen. 2:9–14

This is a wonderful description of a real place called the Garden of Eden, and even gives its location with some geographic features known to us today.

> *"Then the Lord God took the man and put him into the garden of Eden to cultivate it and keep it."* Gen. 2:15

Adam now has his first creative opportunity, and it is a task involving work. One teacher has called Adam a "weed puller." We can debate whether weeds as we know them would even be in such a perfect place as the Garden of Eden, but we do know there were things to do, i.e., to "cultivate it and keep it," and Adam was the man called to do whatever that was. I believe this is a pivotal understanding. Why would a created paradise even have work to do in it? Could it be that God might have deliberately ordered things so that Adam could have something on which to exercise his creative powers? This would not have been possible if the Garden were perfect and untouchable, a view that might come to mind from Sunday School lessons.

Could it be, and this is a point not to miss, that God made Adam in such a way that he could also exercise his own creativity on the world around him? We recognize that man was endowed from the beginning with free will. In a paradise setting where sin had not affected his thought process, the choices Adam made were new *and good*. He is now about to receive his second creative opportunity:

> *"And out of the ground the Lord God formed every beast of the field and every bird of the sky, and brought them to the man to see what he would call them; and whatever the man called a living creature, that was its name."* Gen. 2:19

God has now given Adam a second opportunity to exercise the knowledge and abilities he was created with: to name all the animals. This, I believe, involved more than just a name, but rather a body of knowledge and observations about each creature, and he wasn't just making scratches on cave walls! Adam was a sinless man with all his intellectual abilities and physical energies intact.

The phrase ". . . and He brought them to the man to see what he would call them" could be a little theological minefield, but we will look at the phrase as pleasure expressed by God to witness the co-creative abilities He had given Adam to express knowledge that hadn't existed on earth until now.

Mankind seems to know about itself that it has the ability and drive to make and/or think of things that weren't there before.[4] Before the Fall, that ability would have been at its zenith. And the place given to Adam to do that was Eden, where we can imagine there were boundless opportunities to think and do and arrange in ways that only pleased God.

From this, we see that in the space of barely 15 verses, man is created, put in his place of dwelling, given a description of it and its location, told to work his creative powers on it to cultivate it and keep it, and then to use his "unfallen" mind to create a body of knowledge about every creature on earth! This is a very tight, brief sequence of verses that has nothing in it except Adam's coming into being and what he is to do with his life, namely, work.

We need to note that wrapped around verse 19 is the whole description of the need for and creation of Eve. God makes the declaration that Adam should not be alone and then gives him a helper. So, was it a companion that God gave him, or a helper? Over the ages, societies have sometimes interpreted that to be one or the other, either a companion or helper. I suggest it is both. She is Adam's helper and she is his companion. The fact that Adam already was created for and had an assignment for work implies the need for a helper. Helpers are only needed if there is work to do. What God had in mind about procreation without her, only He knows. Could it be that He really meant that Adam *cannot* be alone? We do know that at some point after that, things went downhill fast.

THE FALL

When the Fall occurred, the curse itself speaks almost entirely of the nature of work from that time on. It says nothing about who or what Adam is to be, *only how his work is affected:*

> *"Cursed is the ground because of you;*
> *In toil you will eat of it*

---

4. "Man is never himself except when he is actively creating something." Dorothy Sayers, *Creed or Chaos*.

All the days of your life.
Both thorns and thistles it shall grow for you;
And you will eat the plants of the field;
By the sweat of your face
You shall eat bread,
Till you return to the ground,
Because from it you were taken;
For you are dust,
And to dust you shall return." Gen. 3:17b–19

This is the division between that blessed communion with God during which Adam and Eve were able to talk face to face with their Creator, drink in the sensual beauties of the Garden, taste of the fruit and nuts that were theirs to pick that were ripened perfectly without toil on their part, go about with physical vigor we can only dream about, and live in a perfect harmony with the animal kingdom. The curse takes a mere 70 words. As a result of this curse:

". . . therefore the Lord God sent him out from the garden
of Eden, to cultivate the ground from which he was taken."
Gen. 3:23

Adam's exit instructions on leaving the Garden are only to continue working, in this case tilling the ground. However, working conditions have changed drastically. He must now work just to supply himself with the essentials of life. The phrase "tilling the ground" obviously includes all gainful work. During the age of the patriarchs, before and just after the Flood, folks were identified by the types of work they did, as other occupations came into being. Nowhere during this time is any ecclesiastical or political office such as prophet, priest, or king mentioned. There is not one word on how to organize society, form a worship group, or assign certain people to intercede before God. Here are a couple of passages about occupations:

"And Abel was a keeper of flocks, but Cain was a tiller of the
ground." Gen. 4:2

"And Adah gave birth to Jabal; he was the father of those who dwell in tents and have livestock. And his brother's name was Jubal; he was the father of all those who play the lyre and pipe. As for Zillah, she also gave birth to Tubal-cain, the forger of all implements of bronze and iron; . . ." Gen. 4:20–22a

THE CURSE OF CAIN

In the dialogue between God and Cain after the murder of Abel, God pronounces an additional curse on Cain that, you guessed it, has to do with Cain's ability to do work.

"When you cultivate the ground, it shall no longer yield its strength to you; you shall be a vagrant and a wanderer on the earth." Gen. 4:12

God has now pronounced an additional curse on Cain. Cain is so chagrined at this double curse on his ability to do work that he wails, "My punishment is greater than I can bear (for) surely You have driven me this day from the face of the ground." He knows he is called to do work and *wants* to work but is no longer able to do so by decree from God. He is not executed; he is not put in prison. In fact, he is free to roam the earth but without any productive abilities or purpose. God in His mercy even provides for his safety as a fugitive. Cain's only punishment is that there is nothing productive he can do now. *He can't think of a greater punishment on this earth.* Mankind is made to do things. The worst sentence God can pronounce on him is to forbid productive, creative work.

In the process of the Fall, man's creative power, that is, his ability to bring forth something new and good, was seriously compromised. He now had to expend considerable energy just to feed and clothe himself. More importantly, his mind was now given over to outright rebellion against God, and he even questioned whether God was the Creator at all!

By the time of the Flood, man had sought after every conceivable degenerative thought and action, for as God observed, "man was filled with every evil thought continually." Even so, in the midst of this worldwide debauchery and rebellion against His created order, God still insists on going back to His original plan for us in the Creation. That plan was for us to continue working.

THE FLOOD

After mankind had come to a state of complete deprivation, God chose the Flood as the method of destruction. The person appointed to provide for the preservation of mankind was Noah, the builder of the Ark that saved mankind through the Flood. His very name identifies him with the concept of work:

> *"Now He called his name Noah saying, 'This one shall give us rest from (literally, comfort us in) our work and from the toil of our hands, arising from the ground which the Lord has cursed.'"* Gen. 5:29

A strict translation of his name "Noah," or the Hebrew *Noakh*, means "rest." Have you ever thought, or were you ever taught, that Noah's prime call was to "give us rest from our work"? Just how we attained rest from our work through Noah's role is unclear; however, the King James Version, New King James Version, and New American Standard Bible use the word "comfort." That understanding gives us a bit more wiggle room theologically to see the strength of God's promise immediately after the Flood and the central place work has in God's plan for mankind. After the water had subsided, the Ark had landed, the animals released, and a burnt offering made, the first words out of the Lord's mouth spoke of rainbows, right? Wrong. No more floods? Wrong.

> *". . . I will never again curse the ground on account of man . . ."* Gen. 8:21

Yes, Noah and his family were physically saved so there would be a new people on the earth, but for what? Could it be so that we could continue our work, the reason God created us? Without any pun intended, it was so we could hit the ground running. On with it! There's work to do! In Noah's case, there were vineyards to plant.

God has consistently, from the very beginning, used productive, creative work as a major theme around which He has conducted Himself and orchestrated the purposes and gifting of mankind. He has identified Himself with work, created man for and defined his role by work, pronounced curses that make work harder, and saved us through the Flood so our work could continue.

STUDY QUESTIONS

1. What scriptural evidence do we have that productive work for man was a central part of God's thinking from the beginning?
2. What subject takes up most of the narrative of God's curse on Adam after the Fall?
3. In Genesis 2:15, God puts Adam into the Garden of Eden to cultivate it and keep it. Discuss the implications of that statement for us today.
4. Discuss the difference between the curse on Adam and the curse on Cain.
5. How is Noah linked to the concept of work?

Chapter Two
The Decline
of Work[5]

"And Adah gave birth to Jabal; he was the father of those
who dwell in tents and have livestock."

Gen. 4:20

W E HAVE JUST TAKEN A JOURNEY through the sequence of the Creation of the world and of man. The overarching purpose for man's
existence as described in the first few chapters of Genesis is to work
alongside God in bringing beauty and order to the Garden by "culti-
vating it and keeping it."

But, you say, "Wasn't it beautiful and orderly and fertile and
lush already?" Good question, but the answer has to be a resound-
ing, "Yes!" What was there for us to do then? What needs to be
done in a perfect place? Maybe nothing. Nothing that *needs* to be

---

5. The dates used herein will be from Archbishop Ussher's calendar constructed
from his *The Annals of the World* and as printed in the margins of The King James
Version of the Bible. I am aware that modern scholarship has questioned the
Archbishop's approach of taking dates from the Bible itself and working backward.
This may, in fact, not be absolutely correct, but for our singular need to put time
perspective on the various events, we will use his dating for that purpose.

done, anyway, but many pleasing things *could* be done for God's good pleasure. If it is beautiful and orderly already, what could man do to improve on it? Again, the answer has to be, "probably nothing."

So we will go in this intellectual loop forever unless we allow for a different thought, and that thought is this: God wanted to see what *other* beauties might come out of the mind of this creature into which He had put His own breath, namely Man, and He might not know what exactly that would be! Creating, even as a co-creator, carries monumental overtones for us, because it speaks to the character of God and of the possibilities He gave Man to think and act.

THE TIMELINE OF WORK

What we want to do now is survey the mention of occupations in the patriarchal period to get an idea of the types of work done in this time span. We want to see how the people in this period were identified, and we also want to notice things that were not mentioned about them.

3875 BC—Cain and Abel had occupations. All we know about them is that ". . . Abel was a keeper of flocks, but Cain was a tiller of the ground."[6] Cain was what we would call a cash crop farmer, i.e., one who grew grain to eat or sell. Abel grew livestock. This was their work. The Bible says nothing else about what they did or how they were identified. The fact of their occupations is apparently all we need to know about them and is the most important thing about them.

3750 BC—There is an amazing description in Genesis 4:19–22 of very ordinary occupations in the sixth generation after Cain. A list of the skills and occupations of the sons of Lamech is given. Why the Bible waits until several generations after Adam before mentioning these trades by name is not clear. Perhaps

---

6. Gen. 4:2.

these men were particularly skilled in what they did, or had refined their skills to a high level, or what they were doing had just been perfected.

On the surface of it, there are simple word descriptions of what they were; however, each one requires subsets of skills and occupations to keep the main one going—and it's interesting to think about them. They include farming of livestock by Jabal, something we already knew about with Abel. That requires the building of shelters, butchering abilities, shearers, shearing tools, the ability to make garments from the skins and fleece, and tent making, since Jabal lived in tents. We usually think of some kind of fabric for tents; therefore, weavers and someone had to design and make a loom or spinning wheel.

Then there is Jubal, the father of those who play the lyre and pipe. Musicians must obviously have music, either written by themselves or someone else. Having the music requires a substance to write the music on and write with, and a woodworker to make instruments such as lyres and pipes.

And then we come to Tubal-Cain, a forger of implements of bronze and iron. That begs for a whole bevy of skills and talents, starting with a knowledge of and skill in mining, smelting, tool making, alloying knowledge (bronze), and a market for whatever those products were. This was not a society of grunting cave dwellers! Am I speaking as a businessperson would? Yes, and I am apparently in good company!

Incidentally, scholars have revealed that the skill of ironworking was lost for centuries after the Flood, until about 1500 BC. Anthropologists call this the "Iron Age." This speaks volumes to those of us who are tempted to think of antediluvian (pre-Flood) society as being very primitive. Already, within 200 years after the Creation, men were employing skills that were not recovered until 850 years after the Flood!

In all of this, many had to don the hat of teacher and mentor for all of the skills mentioned. Notice there is no mention in the scriptural narrative about political or ecclesiastical offices during this age.

2347 BC—Just to build the Ark, Noah had to have amazing skills in logging, structural knowledge, milling, and the writing down of somewhat detailed engineering drawings on construction of the Ark. All we have recorded is that God gave him the basic dimensions, but probably didn't send along a set of detailed drawings! A covered vessel 450 feet long and 45 feet high—with 3 decks and hundreds of cages and provender for everything and everyone—doesn't just come into being by itself. Noah was a vintner after the Flood, and may have been one before. Also, can you imagine the body of knowledge Noah and his sons may have carried with them in the Ark? Based on our previous observation about the loss of metalworking skills for several centuries after the Flood, that was apparently not a particular piece of knowledge he brought with him!

1921 BC—Abraham is the person God chose to found a nation that would be a redemptive bridge between God and fallen mankind. He was given a promise that "...in you shall all the families of the earth be blessed."[7] It is his life around which the entire plan of redemption is pivoted. His occupation was that of a wealthy rancher. *Now Abram was very rich in livestock, in silver and in gold.*[8]

He also served as a provider and protector for other folks beyond his family, for it says, *And Abram took Sarai his wife and Lot his nephew, and all their possessions which they had accumulated, and the persons which they had acquired in Haran, and they set out for the land of Canaan...*[9] This is a model for some who are leaders and have the means and the temperament to positively affect the security of those around them. Abram didn't reject these people. Some may have been slaves, and some had attached themselves

---

7. Gen. 12:3.
8. Gen. 13:2.
9. Gen. 12:5.

to him for the provision and safety of their families. This can also be a part of the call God puts on certain people.

1490 BC—When the Ten Commandments were given, the Fourth Commandment was seen as a validation of the day of rest, which it certainly was, but it also says "six days you shall labor and do all your work...." It is a command from God that we work. Note that for Adam in the Garden, it was his privilege to work. Cain, his son, was chagrined that he could no longer do productive work. By the time the Commandments were given, we had to be reminded and commanded to work.

1462 BC—There is a very important list of occupations in Exodus that has the unique quality of being the description of one man, Bezalel. He was the chief craftsman in building the Tabernacle in the desert during the time of wandering of the people of Israel. It is an exquisite and beautiful design that was also portable, and was made according to God's directions. It was for the purpose of worshipping God Himself and so must have had a high degree of skill and precision brought to bear on its execution. Here is how this is described. There will be several observations to be made about this somewhat lengthy narrative:

> "See, I have called by name Bezalel, the son of Uri, the son of Hur, of the tribe of Judah. I have filled him with the Spirit of God in wisdom, in understanding, in knowledge, and in all kinds of craftsmanship, to make artistic designs for work in gold, in silver, and in bronze, and in the cutting of stones for settings, and in the carving of wood, that he may work in all kinds of craftsmanship.
>
> "And behold, I Myself have appointed with him Oholiab, the son of Ahisamach, of the tribe of Dan; and in the hearts of all who are skillful I have put skill, that they may make all that I have commanded you: the tent of meeting, and the ark of testimony, and the mercy seat upon it, and all the furniture of the tent, the table also and its utensils, and the pure gold lamp stand with all its utensils, and the altar of incense, the altar of burnt offering also with all its utensils, and the

laver and its stand, the woven garments as well, and the holy garments for Aaron the priest, and the garments of his sons, with which to carry on their priesthood; the anointing oil also, and the fragrant incense for the holy place, they are to make them according to all that I have commanded you.[10]

Because of the special nature of the building being undertaken, God filled Bezalel and Oholiab with understanding of many different crafts at once, by the *Spirit of God.* It may have come as close as fallen man has ever been to the creative and skilled atmosphere in the Garden of Eden. Notice however that this anointing applied *". . . in the hearts of all who are skillful I have put skill."* This, then, is not limited to a few craftsmen who lived 1400 years before Christ. None of us are excluded from this promise and empowerment. We can all believe this for ourselves, and you may know of many who exercise their occupations in this way. Perhaps you already consider yourself anointed to do the work you are engaged in!

Interestingly enough, from this time on, people were seldom identified by their occupations, except as priests and kings. When the people of Israel rebelled at Mt. Sinai, demanding the golden calf at the very moment when God was speaking order into their lives through Moses and the Ten Commandments, they abrogated their role as priests to the nations and required God to appoint a system that provided for their own intercession.

Observations

From this historical timeline of the Old Testament up to the time of the Exodus, several observations can be made that bear on our subject of Work as given to us by God:

1. Everyone in this time period was identified by his or her occupation, or work vocation.
2. Neither our creativity nor our ability to make choices was canceled at the Fall, although both began to be used for wrong

---

10. Exod. 31:2–6.

purposes. Notice the attitude of Lamech, the father of the three pioneering men, Jabal, Jubal, and Tubal-Cain. He was a belligerent and forceful man, boasting of killing a man for injuring him. The moral climate was deteriorating quickly.

3. Man's need for useful work was not canceled at the Fall, although his desire and ability to do it began to falter. This became the root of laziness, slothfulness, and gluttony.

4. Contrary to a common perception, the antediluvian societies were populated by highly skilled people who knew techniques not recovered until many centuries after the Flood.

5. Even in our fallen state, we can call for and expect God to fill us with all wisdom and knowledge to perform that particular task the Lord has given us.

The Timeline of Thinking

We will now take this journey through time again from the moment just after the Flood (2350 BC) to the beginning of the Age of Philosophy in 600 BC. This time, we will look for the pattern of deterioration in man's attitude about work.

2250 BC: The Tower of Babel—In describing the fourth generation after Shem, Genesis 10:25 says: *"Two sons were born to Eber; the name of the one was Peleg, for in his days the earth was divided; and his brother's name was Joktan."* The name Peleg means "division." If, therefore, Babel occurred during Peleg's life, it would be about 100 years after the Flood, or 2250 BC. Confusion and worldly thinking took hold of mankind from that time. Although the narrative of what happened at Babel takes place in Genesis 11, the so-called Table of Nations is in the previous chapter, Chapter Ten, and lists the genealogy after Noah and the directions to which they were scattered. This included the eastern migration to China and Southeast Asia, something we Greek-thinking Westerners tend to forget. These civilizations will develop their own societal structures, but will all have layers of stratification that sort out what kind of physical labor each will have to do.

1920 BC: The Call of Abraham from Ur of the Chaldees, a society of moon worshippers, is described in Genesis 12:1–3:

"Now the LORD said to Abram,
'Go forth from your country,
And from your relatives
And from your father's house,
To the land which I will show you;
And I will make you a great nation,
And I will bless you,
And make your name great;
And so you shall be a blessing;
And I will bless those who bless you,
And the one who curses you I will curse
And in you all the families of the earth will be blessed.'"

These are truly pivotal verses of the Bible. The first eleven chapters of Genesis describe the history of the world from the Creation to several hundred years after the Flood. Chapter Twelve begins the great redemption narrative. It lasts from here to the end of the Bible and describes the plan our Lord put in place after the apostasy and corrupt thinking of the first 2,000 years of history. Secular historians would say Abraham was originally from the "cradle of civilization" in what is now Iraq, between the Tigris and Euphrates rivers. The building and construction arts were flourishing there already, as well as agriculture. Abraham lived 4,000 years ago, at the dawn of civilization as we know it. Ziggurats are some of the earliest buildings in one of the earliest identified societies, and Abraham lived during that time. In fact, a straight reading of biblical chronology would show that Shem, the son of Noah, was still living when Abraham was born. It's not a stretch to believe Abraham may have known him and heard a firsthand account of God's intervention at the Flood. Interesting thought. We will now note several mileposts of history that took place after Abraham's life that include the formation of several major religions identifiable today.

2400–1800 BC: The Beginning of Hinduism—There are many scholarly opinions about the formation of this religion. One theory is that it had its roots in Europeans of Aryan blood; another, that it arose in the Indus River Valley in modern-day Pakistan. It does seem to have formed soon after the Flood.

1700 BC—The Egyptian Sojourn of the Israelites followed a severe famine in the Middle East. This is an example of one of the most stark societal contrasts in history. The Israelites were enslaved as an entire nation, not by those who were thinking about God, or contemplating God (terms we will encounter later), but by the Pharaoh, a man who thought he was God himself!

1490 BC: Exodus from Egypt by the Israelites and the Giving of the Ten Commandments at Mt. Sinai—A major feature of this Law is the total absence of earthly political or ecclesiastical office, except for the later appointment of Judges. Everyone else is on a level playing field. It even provides for the forgiving of debts every 49 years so that no person could permanently lord it over another economically. God's law has no societal layers.

1050–950 BC: Israel's Golden Years—The wealth, geographic footprint, and military might of Israel were at their peak during the reigns of David and Solomon. However, these are worldly measures of success, and they ultimately brought on physical conflict externally and spiritual conflict internally that eventually caused the downfall of Israel as a nation. In addition, these two kings fulfilled the warning of the prophet Samuel to the people of Israel when they demanded a king rather than the Judges God provided for them: that their sons and daughters would be conscripted into the king's service, and that a tenth of their best property, flocks, and servants would be confiscated. God's best plan never includes the layering of society.

586 BC: Apostasy and Exile—In this year, the people of Judah were taken captive to Babylon by King Nebuchadnezzar. It was during this time that the prophet Jeremiah delivered a word to the Jewish exiles in Chapter Twenty-nine of his book that will be

discussed later. In it, he gives them rules of behavior when living in a foreign land, and for our purposes, the exhortation to work to support themselves.

630–330 BC: Rise of Man-Made Religions and Philosophies
Buddhism—founder, Siddartha Gautama, a.k.a. The Buddha
The Tao—founder, Lao Tsu
Confucianism—founder, Kong Fuzi, a.k.a. Confucius
Greek Philosophy—primarily Socrates, Plato, and Aristotle
The first three of these were formed around the thoughts and life of one man and are called the "Eastern religions." At the risk of oversimplification, we may say that the Eastern religions all teach hard work, good ethics, and kindness to others. It is the Western (Greek) philosophy that assumes slavery and virtually defined the two-tiered work environment that we now call "dualism," and it is from within this system that Christianity was founded.

Whether it's a coincidence or not, I find it interesting that many of the world religions began not long after Israel's apostasy. It's almost as if a restrainer was gone.

(See "Major Religions & Philosophies," Appendix A.)

By the time of the Greek philosophers (600–300 BC), man's understanding and appreciation of creative, vocational work in the West had become completely perverted. It was considered a dishonor to have to do physical labor, and work was relegated to second-class status. This we shall now pursue in more detail.

STUDY QUESTIONS

1. Discuss the theological overtones of mankind being co-creators with God.
2. What were the distinguishing descriptions of the people living within a few generations of the Creation? What was always mentioned? What was never mentioned?
3. What are the two things the Fourth Commandment directs us to do?

4. Bezalel and Oholiab were the chief craftsmen in the building of the tabernacle. What promise does God give to every craftsman working on that project? How does that affect us today?
5. The reigns of Kings David and Solomon are sometimes referred to as Israel's golden years. How did Samuels's prophesy about the habits of a king describe the ushering in of societal dualism under a monarchy?

Chapter Three
Work Defined Down

"The Greeks couldn't get away from the concept of 'dualism'—
the idea of higher and lower planes of ideas and activities."

John Beckett

T his chapter contains what I consider the heart of the matter in how the thought life of man went from work as a gift to be a co-creator with God to the drudgery and, yes, curse that many of us see it being today. That's a big slide, as it takes us from the bliss of the Garden to, in the worst case, the enslavement of other men to do the work for us. In this latter case, work came to be defined as active, physical labor—the type things we need to do just to sustain our physical beings.

This has a direct connection to the condition in which Adam found himself after the Fall and expulsion from the Garden of Eden. He had to work by the sweat of his brow to grow his crops that had previously been provided just for the picking in the Garden.

As man began to depart from his worship of a Creator God after the Flood, he entered into a self-centered focus on who he was and what he was to do. He forgot that God had created and equipped him for work, that is, to exercise all his special and unique combination of gifts, integrating every part of his life into a process that brings glory to God. Man therefore came to the conclusion, not surprisingly, that he was the center of all things and could do and decide what he wanted without regard for the Creator's call on his life.

Over the next 2,000 years, until the time of the Greek philosophers in about 400 BC, a major change began to take place. Instead of receiving the whole of work as an honorable charge from God, man slowly began to crowd the physical side of work out of the place where thinking and creating happened, and relegated it to a lower place. People began to perceive work as the dull, mostly physical side of life, whereas the thinking and supposedly creative part of our life was separated out to a different, higher plane, at least in the mind of man. In reality, the fact that God worked and assigned both physical (tending the Garden) and intellectual (naming the animals) work to Adam is hardly fodder for believing any part of work to be on a lower plane of activity.

As the Society of Man passed along the timeline from the Flood to the Greeks, it passed through the sad, exilic time of the Jews, as they were driven from their homeland by conquering armies and were carried off to Babylon in 586 BC. As an interesting interlude from the inexorable perversion of thinking about our calling to work, God spoke to the exiles through the prophet about their responsibilities in the alien land in very plain but profound simplicity.

> *"Build houses and live in them; and plant gardens and eat their produce. Take wives and become the fathers of sons and daughters, and take wives for your sons and give your daughters to husbands, that they may bear sons and daughters; and multiply there and do not decrease. And seek the welfare of the city where I have sent you into exile, and pray to the LORD on its behalf; for in its welfare you will have welfare."*[11]

This timeless exhortation from the prophet contains a very direct list of responsibilities for the exiles that are now living in an alien land.

---

11. Jer. 29:5–7.

Their behavior could have taken a very different turn, given their circumstances and probably sour attitude, having just been dragged from their homeland by force. The commands are a model for us, to not get fancy with our life and purpose by ignoring basic responsibilities, if you will. Those of us who call on the Lord in this day are also aliens in a foreign land, so to speak, and in spite of our circumstances, the exhortations are the same: to build, provide for yourself, marry, multiply, and seek the good of our city. There are no stump speeches about politics, revenge, pity parties, or of who is on top by Jeremiah. "Just get busy and do it!" he said. The undertone of working hard is not difficult to infer.

Here is a point to be made. Any time the laws and rules for society are laid down by God, there are no layers, no stratification, no dualism, no politics, and always work. Consider the three examples we have mentioned. First the Creation, second the giving of the Law, and third, the commands to the Exiles.

First, as explained in Chapter One at Creation, Adam was created to work, his work was cursed at the Fall, and civilization was saved for the continuation of its work at the Flood. There is no mention in this part of Genesis of government or even ecclesiastical offices. People are only known by their work.

Second, as described in Chapter Two, in the giving of the Law, we were commanded to work six days of the week in the Third Commandment (how we love to focus on that one day of rest provided for). The subsequent expansion of these commandments recorded in Leviticus is notorious for the absence of government and societal layers.

Third, as just described, the exiles in Babylon were told to work to provide for themselves and work for the good of the city they were in. There is a distinct thread in these narratives of lack of societal stratification and the command to work. God's thinking is plainly revealed here, and it has not changed.

As we continue our journey through time, we now pick up how the rest of the world's civilizations continue this decline into a tiered hierarchal society. This took many paths in different cultures in scattered parts of the earth from the East in China and India to the progenitor of our own thought life in the West, the Greeks.

GREECE

By the time of the Greek philosophers, who lived from 1000–300 BC, the attitude toward work in the West was that it had become nothing more than a blot on our life of contemplation and acquisition of knowledge. "To the Greeks, work was a curse and nothing else" and "to be out of work was a piece of singular good fortune."[12]

According to the Greeks, the true way to God was to contemplate Him, to emotionally and intellectually try to connect with Him. Doing heroics of a military or artistic sort also emulated what they thought the characteristics of God to be. This didn't leave much time to do the physical work required to fill the biological needs of the human body, a lower function anyway, so slaves were the answer. Greeks of the day didn't spend much time on apologetics for the idea of slavery; it was just the accepted norm, no problem. Slavery was an entrenched institution during this period and was defended by the philosophers, especially Aristotle, who observed that some human beings were less than fully human and, therefore, were slaves by nature. It's not hard to see how two "classes" of human activity came to be. The lower class had to work physically and to conduct commerce; the others gave themselves to thought, art, and heroic deeds.

Some have already written on the subject of dualism and the effect this kind of thinking has had on the church through the ages. In very recent times, thinking men and women have grappled with what they increasingly see as a flawed and wounded body of belief in the church on who "lay" people are, and what they are to do. The separation of form and matter by Plato, and the incorporation of the Greek way of thinking into the church itself, has transformed the created order of work by God and His assignments to us to continue to "till the ground" and to "tend the garden," i.e., to engage in commercial activity, into something that is on a lower plane.

Here is how John Beckett puts it. "The Greeks couldn't get away from the concept of 'dualism'— the idea of higher and lower planes of ideas and activities. Plato was the clearest on this. He sought to

---

12. Lee Hardy, *The Fabric of This World*, Grand Rapids, MI, Wm. B. Eerdmanns Publishing Company, 1990, p. 7.

identify unchanging universal truths, placing them in the higher of two distinct realms. This upper level he called 'form,' consisting of eternal ideas. The lower level he called 'matter.' This lower realm was temporal and physical. Plato's primary interest lay in the higher form. He deemed it superior to the temporary and imperfect world of matter. The rub comes when we see where Plato placed work and occupations. Where, indeed? In the lower realm."[13] Platonic dualism strikes at the heart of the work of the Creator God, as Nancy Pearcy says, "... by identifying the source of chaos and evil with some part of God's creation, namely matter. Creation was divided into two parts: the spiritual (superior, good) and the material (inferior, bad).

"This stands in clear opposition to the biblical worldview, which teaches that nothing exists from eternity over against God. Matter is not some preexisting stuff with its own independent properties, capable of resisting God's power. God created it and thus has absolute control over it. This was the operative meaning of the doctrine of creation ex nihilo (creation out of nothing)—that nothing is independent of God, but everything came from Him and is subject to Him.

"In contrast to the Greeks then, the Bible presents the material world as originally good: Since it was created by God, it reflects His good character. The Bible does not identify evil with matter or with any other part of creation, but with sin, which twists and distorts God's originally good creation. For example, Scripture does not treat the body as inherently sinful or less valuable. When Paul urges us in Galatians 5 to avoid 'the lusts of the flesh,' he is not referring to the body but is using 'flesh' as a technical term for the sinful nature. Indeed, if the body were inherently sinful, the Incarnation would have been impossible, for Jesus took on a human body yet had no sin. The sheer monumental fact that God Himself took on human form speaks decisively of the dignity of the body. For Greek thinkers, the most shocking claim Christians made was that God had become a historical person, who could be seen, heard, and touched. Rational inquiry could no longer simply reject the world of the senses but had

---

13. John Beckett, *Loving Monday*, Downers Grove, IL, Intervarsity Press, 1998, p. 67.

to take account of history—events in time and space like Christ's incarnation, death, and resurrection.

"Another way to put it is that Scripture defines the human dilemma as moral—the problem is that we have violated God's commands. But the Greeks defined the human dilemma as metaphysical—the problem is that we are physical, material beings. And if the material world is bad, then the goal of the religious life is to avoid, suppress, and ultimately escape from the material aspects of life. Manual labor was regarded as less valuable than prayer and meditation."[14]

CHINA

The Chinese put in place an examination system to identify literate "presented gentlemen," or *jinshi*. They were known as the SHI, pronounced "shir." It was a civil service system, if you will, but rather than just a pass/fail at a lower level, as we have in the United States, it was designed to aggressively sort out the brightest and best in stages lasting several years until those that survived at the top were fit to serve the Emperor himself. At that level, they were multilingual and proficient in the arts, sciences, and politics.

The Confucian exams, as these came to be known, had been used in a minor role to supplement the "recommendation" system from the Han Dynasty of 205 BC–AD 200. They were gradually enhanced up to the Song Dynasty of AD 970–1250. Following were some basic guidelines:

Qualified for Exams
1. From established, elite families—the literati
2. Artisans
3. Farmers

Not Qualified for Exams
1. Women
2. Small "outcast" groups
3. Merchants and their sons—they lived off the efforts of others

---

14. Nancy Pearcy, *Total Truth*, Wheaton, IL, Crossway Books, 2005, p. 76.

It's one thing to sort out the most able candidates to serve in public roles through a series of examinations, all the way up to the staff of the emperor, but to disqualify some from even entering the exam system belies a dualistic system of thinking, even in this culture.

INDIA

In India, the Hindus are well known for their caste system, which divides society into four main groups known as Varna; this refers to the categorization of the Hindu society as four castes. This system was hypothesized by Brahmins, who, of course, put themselves in the highest caste. The four Varnas are described in the following stratified order, from top to bottom:

- Brahmins: Scholars, teachers, and fire priests
- Kshatriyas: Kings and warriors
- Vaishyas: Agriculturists and merchants
- Shudras: Service providers and artisans

Separate and shunned by the society are the "Untouchables," who have to deal with the disposal of dead bodies and human waste and are described as dirty and polluted by those in the other castes. Predictably, those who work for a living, including merchants, are in the bottom two categories. Notice that the Chinese placed artisans among the elite; the Indians had them at the bottom.

This brief description of three major societies is enough to display what happens when fallen man contrives to organize himself away from anarchy and chaos. The inevitable result is a system of layers, tiers, or castes that typically place merchants and physical laborers at the bottom, and everyone else above them. The ultimate "game changer" is about to appear in time, and the world will never be the same.

STUDY QUESTIONS

1. Discuss work as God created it to be versus what man ended up with by the time of the Greek philosophers.

2. What things are absent from societies living according to God's laws? Give three examples.
3. What is Dualism as lived by the Greeks in 400 BC?
4. What three major societies are discussed in this chapter that exhibited a system of societal layers? Discuss one of them.

Chapter Four
The Christ Effect

"He has brought down the rulers from their thrones, and has
exalted those who were humble."

Luke 1:52

INTO THE MAN-MADE SYSTEM OF HIERARCHY, layers, social strata,
and the wielding of power over others in every society on earth, Jesus
Christ came to set us free. A major part of His purpose on earth was,
among other things, to set us free from the bondage of man-made
systems. It's impossible to overemphasize the impact He made on
this subject, for what He said and did flies in the face of the dualism
existing in virtually every society at that time and, as it turns out, was
a lot different than what the church came to be after His ascension.

First, Jesus's entry into this world took place in a very modest
and unassuming way that left out those in the higher strata of society. His mother was of "humble estate," by her own admission. After
learning she was to become pregnant by the Holy Spirit, she uttered
her sublime Magnificat, which contained these words that are the
core of her prophecy: "He has scattered those who were proud in the
thoughts of their heart. He has brought down the rulers from their

thrones, and has exalted those who were humble. He has filled the hungry with good things; and sent away the rich empty handed."[15]

How many times in my life have I almost passed over that part of Mary's song, not realizing what a large part of His ministry she was describing? From before He was born, His human mother declared prophetically that a major part of His task on this earth was to eliminate the man-made strata that had permeated every society of peoples. His ministry was not just to raise up the lowly; rather, it was to utterly disassemble the layers we had created for ourselves, so we could start over on a level playing field.

Second, the announcement of His birth was worthy of a heavenly king, made by legions of angels, but was made only to lowly shepherds working the night shift. His first crib was a donkey's feed box.

Third, Jesus spent a great amount of time speaking against burdens the rulers of the synagogue had laid on the people. It began with John the Baptist, who minced no words when speaking to the rulers of the church: "You brood of vipers, who warned you to flee from the wrath to come? Therefore bring forth fruit in keeping with your repentance; and do not suppose that you can say to yourselves, 'We have Abraham for our father'; for I say to you, that God is able from these stones to raise up children to Abraham."[16] In other words, John was giving fair warning that Jesus was not going to be impressed with titles or even heritage. He wanted to see a repentant heart and the accompanying fruit, or good works that would verify what is in our heart. He is, after all, primarily interested in what is in our heart. *This is never truer than in our work life.*

The heart we bring to the work given to us is a sure sign of the peace imparted by knowing we are in the "sweet spot" of God's will for us and our gifting to do it. Jesus himself uses nearly identical wording when addressing the Pharisees, "You brood of vipers, how can you, being evil, speak what is good?"[17] Although you will seldom

---

15. Luke 1:51–53.
16. Matt. 3:7–9.
17. Matt. 12:34.

hear it said this way, it is a very plain indictment of the church leaders who thought themselves better than their followers.

Fourth, Jesus also spoke about the millennia-long accumulation of ordinances, rules, and traditions by the Jewish Pharisees and scribes in not so gentle language: "You hypocrites, rightly did Isaiah prophesy of you, saying, 'This people honors Me with their lips, but their heart is far away from Me. But in vain do they worship Me, teaching as their doctrines the precepts of men.'"[18] In fact, by this time in history, the expansion of the original commandments in the Torah had included oral traditions that some rabbis considered at a higher level than the Mosaic laws that were written down! Even the term *rabbi* was a later invention.

By contrast, the team of disciples He surrounded Himself with were fishermen, businessmen, and zealots. None were church officials or politicians. He invited Himself into the home of a societal outcast named Zaccheus, who was a tax collector–type businessman.[19] It was commonly understood that people in this profession cheated the citizens by overcharging them for their tax obligation.

He welcomed the little children to be with Him when even His disciples wanted to shoo them away.[20] He demolished both racial and gender discrimination in one conversation with a Samaritan woman.[21] He reached out to the down-and-outers such as beggars, prostitutes, ailing widows, and the lame with healing and demonic deliverance. He dined in the home of a leper, a person considered untouchable and a societal pariah.[22]

He illustrated pride in a parable, using the example of a Pharisee who prayed loudly about his giving and accomplishments, contrasted with a humble man who prayed quietly in the corner, begging God for forgiveness.[23] He also exhorted His followers to voluntarily go to

---

18. Matt. 15:7–9.
19. Luke 19:1–10.
20. Matt. 19:13–15.
21. John 4:1–14.
22. Mark 14: 3–9.
23. Luke 18:9–14.

the last seat at the banquet rather than push to the head table, "but many who are first will be last; and the last, first."[24]

He illustrated a right attitude in giving, by commending the poor widow for giving her last penny as opposed to the rich man who gave more money but with great fanfare. In other words, He completely demolished the ideas of those who believed they had standing in the eyes of men, and elevated those who had no standing. Everything was reversed. The high were made low, and the low were lifted up.

As a follow-up, the apostle Paul noted that ". . . the foolishness of God is wiser than men, and the weakness of God is stronger than men. For consider your calling brethren, that there were not many wise according to the flesh; not many mighty, not many noble; but God has chosen the foolish things of the world to shame the wise, and God has chosen the weak things of the world to shame the things which are strong, and the base things of the world and the despised God has chosen, the things that are not so that He may nullify the things that are, so that no man may boast before God."[25] In other words, none of us can elevate ourselves above another.

That doesn't mean that some didn't try, for as Paul points out in Galatians 4:17, the Judaizers "eagerly seek you, not commendably, but they wish to shut you out, in order that you may seek them." It sounds convoluted, but there is ecclesiastical manipulation going on here by which the folks in Galatia are courted, but for no good. The ultimate aim of the Judaizers is to make themselves wanted and thereby elevate themselves above the faithful.

He (Paul) also reflected the words of Christ when he said, "There is neither Jew nor Greek, there is neither slave nor free man, there is neither male nor female, for you are all one in Christ Jesus."[26]

He further noted that we should "be of the same mind toward one another, do not be haughty in mind, but associate with the lowly. Do not be wise in your own estimation."[27]

---

24. Matt. 19:30.
25. I Cor. 1:26–29.
26. Gal. 3:28.
27. Rom. 12:16.

And just so we don't get the idea that there is now a new group on top, Paul further elaborates "that you all agree and there be no divisions among you, but you be made complete in the same mind and in the same judgment."[28] The work of Christ made the redemption available to all in equal measure. We are all gifted differently, for sure, but no one is worth more than another. God is equally delighted with each of us, and wants to see what we will do next!

As a matter of fact, an oft-quoted verse is Colossians 3:23: "...whatever you do, *do your work* heartily, as for the Lord rather than for men . . ." Interestingly enough, this follows immediately after a statement about a business setting, exhorting employees (slaves) to obey their employers (masters), and precedes a statement about the consequences of disobedience.

There is ample evidence in the New Testament about how we are to work and conduct ourselves. First of all, the Master called the disciples *out* of their secular work, but trained and mentored them to be apostles, who were in turn to equip the saints for the work of service.

The apostolic exhortations about our daily life and work given in the epistles are amazingly benign in a spiritual sense. II Thessalonians, 3:8-12, contains phrases such as "not eating anyone's bread without paying for it," and "if anyone does not work he shouldn't eat," and that "we should work in a quiet fashion and eat our own bread."

As a result of the redemptive and liberating work of Christ, we are *all* commissioned as priests (again), per I Peter 2:9, which proclaims that we are all part of the "royal priesthood." There *is* a hierarchy *in* the church as laid down in Ephesians 4:11, i.e., apostles, prophets, evangelists, pastors, and teachers. These, however, were put in place to proclaim the Word and equip the saints. The church is doing quite well at proclaiming the evangelistic and personal piety part of the Word. The equipping of the saints, especially for our work in the secular realm, is virtually nonexistent.

What comes to mind is the exhortation from the book of Hebrews to ". . . leave the elementary doctrine of Christ and go on

---

28. I Cor. 1:10.

to maturity, not laying again a foundation of repentance from dead works and faith toward God, and of instructions about washings, the laying on of hands, the resurrection of the dead, and eternal judgment."[29]

That sentence from Hebrews could encompass the total teaching of many of today's churches, even though it is held up by the writer of the book of Hebrews as just the beginning of what the Lord wants us to understand about His will and ways.

For our purposes, we will take up an elaboration of what the church can be doing and teaching about "equipping the saints" in a later chapter. For now, it is our duty to explore the distortions of the words of Christ that began to accumulate very soon after the death of the apostles, the last persons who learned directly from Christ. It's not a pretty picture.

STUDY QUESTIONS

1. What major part of the ministry of Jesus Christ is described in Mary's Magnificat?
2. What utterances did Jesus Christ and John the Baptist make that used identical wording?
3. What two forms of discrimination did Jesus destroy in one conversation? Who was it with?
4. What is the purpose of the hierarchy mentioned in Ephesians 4:11?

---

29. Heb. 6:1–2.

Chapter Five
The Post-Apostolic Age

It is not lawful to baptize or give communion without the
consent of the bishop.

Ignatius

B<small>Y THE END OF THE FIRST</small> century AD, there were already signs that
the enormous changes wrought by the life and work of Christ were
being compromised. For example, the inevitable strange doctrines
and heretical beliefs that popped up caused church leaders to say by
way of protection of the flock, "Wherever the bishop appears, there
let the people be; as wherever Jesus Christ is, there is the Catholic
Church. It is not lawful to baptize or give communion without the
consent of the bishop. On the other hand, whatever has his (the
bishop's) approval is pleasing to God. Thus, whatever is done will be
safe and valid."[30]

This statement by Ignatius unwittingly set in motion the idea that
ordinary believers could and should not presume to assemble before
the Lord without the permission of the bishop. The seeds of dualism

---

30. Ignatius of Antioch, Letter to the Smyrnaeans 8, 68–107 AD, J. R. Willis
Translation.

in the church had been firmly planted. By the fifth century AD, Greek dualism was in full sway in the church. Others, such as Clement of Rome and Cyprian of Carthage, weighed in on the subject.

One of the foremost and formidable thinkers in the post-apostolic era was Augustine of Hippo, who lived in the fifth century AD. He was influenced by Plato and the neo-platonic philosophy. Because he was such an enormous influence on theologians and, therefore, the church, I want to quote Nancy Pearcy on this so we have a handle on the foundations of thinking that in many ways prevails to this day. After dabbling in Manichaeism (there are two gods: one good, the other evil), "…he became a Platonist, then finally converted to Christianity—without however, ever quite giving up all the elements of Platonism. Most important, he retained an adapted notion of the double creation, teaching that God first made the Platonic intelligible Forms, and afterward made the material world in imitation of the Forms.

"The effect of this modified dualism proved devastating. Even though Augustine explicitly affirmed the goodness of creation, his concept of a dual creation had the effect of undercutting what he said and leading to a two-story hierarchy: The immaterial world (the Forms) functioned as his upper story, which he regarded as superior to the material creation on the lower story. 'Despite his averrals of the goodness and reality of the created order,' says theologian Colin Gunton, 'the sensible world (world of senses) is for Augustine manifestly inferior to the intellectual—that Platonic dualism is never long absent from his writing.'

"This dualistic view of creation led naturally to a dualistic view of the Christian life. Thus Augustine embraced an ethic of asceticism, based on the assumption that the physical world and bodily functions were inherently inferior, a cause of sin. The way to reach the higher levels of spiritual life was by renunciation and deprivation of physical wants. He regarded ordinary work in the world, what he called the 'active' life, as inferior to the 'contemplative' life of prayer and meditation shut away in monasteries. He also treated marriage as inferior to celibacy, and even recommended that married clergy not live with their wives!

"Thus, a final distinction has been made between clergy and laymen by conceding to the Greek thought process that marriage and sexuality are part of the material world and therefore inferior for those truly called."[31] Partly because Augustine was such a towering figure in church history, a kind of Christianized Platonism remained the accepted basis of thinking among theologians all the way through the Middle Ages.

By the time Pope Boniface VIII issued the papal Bull Unam Sanctam in AD 1302, the separation of clergy and laity was complete, leaving no doubt that the laity were in second-class status to clergy, monks, and church officials. The Bull laid down dogmatic propositions on the unity of the *Catholic Church*, the necessity of belonging to it for eternal salvation, the position of the Pope as supreme head of the Church, and the duty thence arising of submission to the pope in order to belong to the Church and thus to attain salvation. The Pope further emphasized the higher position of the spiritual in comparison with the secular order.

The twentieth-century Bible teacher A. W. Tozer, who can be counted on to speak plainly, says "That monkish hatred of the body which figures so prominently in the works of certain early devotional writers is wholly without support in the Word of God."[32] Tozer is harking back to those who hold to the Platonic idea of separation of material things from Spiritual. However, such was the hold that Greek dualistic thinking had on the Western mind that the medieval church embraced the tenets of contemplation of God and placed that ahead of acts of service.

The preeminent theologian of the thirteenth century, Thomas Aquinas, states in his *Summa Theologica*, ". . . the contemplation of divine truth is the goal of the whole of human life. This is because the contemplative life is according to that which is most proper to man, namely his intellect. Productive work, which meets the needs of this temporal bodily life, is therefore in itself of no lasting religious

---

31. Nancy Pearcy, *Total Truth*, Wheaton, IL, Crossway Books, 2005, p. 77.
32. A. W. Tozer, *The Pursuit of God*, Camp Hill, PA, Christian Publications, 1993, p 112.

significance. For the most part it hinders the individual's relation to God, which can be cultivated only in the leisure of contemplation."[33]

Did you catch that? The leading theologian of the Dark Ages states that productive work is in itself of no lasting religious significance! How far did we go away from the plain purposes of God when THE spokesman for the church says of work, as a New Yorker might say it: fageddaboudit. "Not only the life of productive work, but even the practical or 'active' life, consisting of virtuous activity directed toward one's neighbor, was seen by many medievals as an impediment to the true goals of the religious life."[34]

On the subject of marriage, Aquinas was somewhat liberated from the early teachings, agreeing that a man should live with his wife (!), but that sex is only for procreation and serves no purpose outside of that goal.

This kind of thinking lasted until the first Reformation. An extreme example of a church steeped in dualism is what we now call the Dark Ages, a part of church history framed, in part, by the type of theological interpretations described here.

In the physical realm, the design of cathedrals then became a prime example of "form follows function," whereby the laity were separated from the altar (they're back now) by a rail, the only ones allowed inside the rail being priests (they're back, too) and bishops.[35] God was far up and unreachable, and the church required priests (again) to intervene for us at an altar. Gothic cathedrals were physically descriptive of our attitude that God was out of reach, beyond the high ceilings.

Reading of the Bible by "lay" persons was forbidden and punishable by torture and death (see *Fox's Book of Martyrs*). The book

---

33. Lee Hardy, *The Fabric of This World*, p. 17.
34. Ibid., p. 18.
35. In reality, this author has seen the ruins of a church at Avdat in the Negev in southern Israel that had an altar and a rail separating the congregation from the officiants. This church was from the fifth century AD! The "freedoms" and legitimacy for Christianity brought by Constantine in AD 313 didn't take long to catch on. This was a Roman army outpost, so the Roman version of Christianity was brought along.

Christian Calling and Vocation by Henlee Barnette is a wonderful summary of this period and was a great resource for me.

A corollary to the separation of the "contemplative" and "active" lives during the Dark Ages was the attitude of the Catholic Church toward doctrines with which it disagreed. There are reasons enough for the Orthodox Church and the Anabaptists to disagree. But the major split in the Orthodox Church in 1054 was caused, in part, by a forged document! The "Donation of Constantine," which had supposedly given temporal powers to the church and caused a rift with the church, was finally proven to be a fraud in 1450.

In the meantime, this document fed the natural desire for power by the Popes and caused an overreach of authority that the Patriarchs of the Eastern Orthodox Church didn't agree with. Therefore, the Roman church solved the problem by excommunicating the Eastern church (and vice versa) on the altar of the Hagia Sophia cathedral in Constantinople in AD 1054, beginning what is known as the "Great Schism."

Likewise, Thomas Aquinas, the foremost theologian of the Middle Ages, spoke of the treatment the Anabaptists should have if they persisted in what were believed to be heretical beliefs. ". . . heresy is a thing for the perpetration of which the guilty one deserves not only to be separated from the Church by excommunication but also *barred from the world by death.*"[36] Although this man had and exercised one of the finest theological minds of the Middle Ages, and helped undo some of the neo-platonism Augustine had brought us into, he still fell prey to theological sophistry that enabled him to make such a statement that brought Christian against Christian.

You might wonder how that could happen. While we are still struggling to get out from under the remains of thoughts like that, we have added some of our own in our day. We will address some of those soon.

---

36. Quoted by Leonard Verduin, *The Reformers and Their Stepchildren*, Grand Rapids, MI, Wm. B. Eerdmanns Publishing Company, 1964, p. 119n.

STUDY QUESTIONS

1. What did Ignatius say that helped precipitate a return to dualism, this time in the church?
2. What is the name of the type of philosophy held by Augustine of Hippo that caused him to believe in a double creation?
3. The "contemplative life" and "active life" are terms used in the Middle Ages to describe a form of what? Name one thing from each category.
4. What type of activity did Thomas Aquinas teach was of no lasting religious significance?

Chapter Six
The Reformation (Almost) of Work

"The second principal question in all religion is whether it must be direct, or mediate."

Abraham Kuyper

I$_N$ THE LAST CHAPTER, WE SAW that before the end of the first century AD, there were signs that the interpretations of man had started to unravel the teachings and intent of Jesus Christ on the subject of what the church is to be and teach. This was nowhere more evident than on the way man relates to man, and how he can come to God. The man-made strata of society that Jesus Christ so effectively destroyed, including the assumptions the church leaders made about themselves, began within a few decades to rear their heads again. This time, it was not the Pharisees and Sadducees of the Jewish synagogues, but the ecclesiastical structure of the New Testament church. We have traced an outline of that in the previous chapter, including the theology of the likes of Ignatius, Augustine, and Aquinas, who set the tone for the thinking that persists in large parts of the church to this day.

MARTIN LUTHER

A major move toward a better understanding of how man can come to and serve God occurred in the sixteenth century as a result of the Reformation begun by Martin Luther. One of the five "solas," or pillars of theology, of the movement is Solo Christo, or salvation through Christ alone. This is a major point of the Reformation and is the teaching that Christ is the only mediator between God and man, and that there is salvation through no other. This principle set the church free from "sacerdotalism," which is the belief that there are no sacraments in the church without the services of priests who are ordained by apostolic succession under the authority of the Pope, and that the sacraments can in fact save us.

"When the Constantinian change was complete, the technique of salvation by Sacrament had effectively replaced the older technique of salvation by the preached Word and its operation on your heart, an internal thing. The logic of salvation by sacramental manipulation leads straight to the idea of *ex opere operato*, the name given to the view that the transaction to which the Sacrament points is 'done in the doing.' In other words, it is the innate power of the Sacrament as the conveyor of grace that assures the mediation of salvation; this rather than the state or the attitude of the dispenser, or the recipient for that matter.

"Sacramentalism also leads to sacerdotalism, which emphasizes the powers of priests as essential mediators between God and mankind to deliver those sacraments. If salvation comes by sacramental manipulation, then the manipulator becomes extremely important; in fact, he becomes indispensable. The Church was extremely jealous of the priestly office, understandably so; for in it was lodged a great potential toward the realization and the perpetuation of 'Christian sacralism' and its hold on the people. The Church created the 'Sacrament of Orders,' an act whereby the power to transubstantiate was allegedly transferred from the officiating priest to the head of the one being ordained. In this way, the Church had its company of trusted officials, its hard core of 'card-carrying party members,' who strictly speaking constitute the *ecclesia*."[37]

---

37. Leonard Verduin, *The Reformers and Their Stepchildren*, Grand Rapids, MI, Wm. B. Eerdmanns Publishing Company, 1964, pp. 140, 141.

We speak of this now because of the implications for our subject of work. Sacerdotalism forced a layer in between God, and you and me. The church effectively said, without that ecclesiastical layer of the officiating priest, you were not saved by your beliefs, no matter how fervently you held to them! You were (are) saved by the administration of certain sacraments by certain people. The other side of the coin is, what you actually believe and do with your life is pushed to the background and doesn't much matter. Remember that phrase, "done in the doing"? When you DO this sacrament, i.e., take it from a priest, you have salvation. No wonder the Mass is so important to a large segment of the church. The Mass has become the *sacrifice* performed by the *priest* standing before an *altar*, all Old Testament concepts.

Martin Luther, on the other hand, taught "the priesthood of all believers," denying the exclusive use of the title "priest" to the clergy. This alone was enough to alienate him from the church authorities of the day, which it did. However, he did not, in the opinion of many, go far enough. According to the teaching of the reformers, the principle of the universal priesthood does not deny the office of the holy ministry, to which is committed the public proclamation of the Gospel and the administration of the sacraments.

Dualism was still alive. The person in this office was a "called and ordained servant of the Word." Luther, in his *Small Catechism*, described the role of a "confessor" to confer sacramental *absolution* on a penitent. The section in this catechism known as "The Office of the Keys" identifies the "called ministers of Christ," or pastors, as being the ones who exercise the binding and loosing of absolution. In this way, the Pastor could forgive penitents' sins by speaking Christ's words of forgiveness—"I forgive you all your sins"—without any addition of penances or satisfactions and not as an interceding or mediating "priest." That's a good thing. The mediating role of priest is now gone, but identifying him as the "called and ordained servant of the Word"[38] is still very much alive and for him, especially in the Lutheran stream of the Protestant world, was reserved the administration of sacraments and of absolution.

---

38. Martin Luther, *Luther's Small Catechism*, St. Louis, MO, Concordia Publishing House, 1943, para. 287.

It was left to Calvin and his followers to completely sever the administration of sacraments from an ecclesiastical layer, for they saw the congregation of believers as self-sufficient to engage in a relationship with the Creator God. Here is how Kuyper puts it:

> *"The second principal question in all religion is whether it must be* direct, *or* mediate. *Must there stand a church, a priest, or as of old, a sorcerer, a dispenser of sacred mysteries, between God and the soul, or shall all intervening links be cast away, so that the bond of religion shall bind the soul directly to God? Now we find that in all non-Christian religions, without any exception, human intercessors are deemed necessary, and in the domain of Christianity itself the intercessor intruded again upon the scene, in the Blessed Virgin, in the host of angels, in the saints and martyrs, and in the priestly hierarchy of the clergy: and although Luther took the field against all priestly mediation, yet the church which is called by his name, renewed by its title of 'ecclesia docens' (teaching church) the office of mediator and steward of mysteries. On this point also it was Calvin, and he alone, who attained to the full realization of the ideal of pure spiritual religion. Religion, as he conceived it, must be without any creaturely intercession, realize the direct communion between God and the human heart."*[39]

On the subject of vocation, Luther and the other reformers did a more complete job of liberation of the "ordinary" Christians. Theologically, he spoke firmly and eloquently about the link between the Creation and the daily work we do— "... the religious significance of human work is first apprehended in the light of the doctrine of creation. *Having fashioned a world filled with resources and potentials, God chose to continue His creative activity in this world through the work of human hands.*"This is an important statement and is worth remembering for our future studies, for not all future theologians will even be able to go there. It was Luther who put back into our minds that

---

39. Abraham Kuyper, *Lectures on Calvinism*, New York, Cosimo Classics, 2007, p. 47.

we were, in fact, participating in the ongoing process of bringing new things and thoughts into being.

On a more basic, daily-life level, he spoke of us being in different "stations" in life, including the type of work we did, our family situation, or level of responsibility over others. He did not believe that it was necessary to abandon our earthly station, even if it be lowly or mundane, for we are working as unto the Lord to serve others at all times. "Our vocation, according to Luther, comes to us through our station. What God would have us do with our time and talents is discerned from the duties which pertain to our stations in life together with the concrete opportunities he has place before us. But what do we accomplish when we discharge the duties of a station in life, when we heed the call of God to serve our neighbor in and through our daily tasks?

"Luther's answer to this question is as astounding as it is humbling: the order of stations in the earthly kingdom has been instituted by God Himself as his way of seeing that the needs of humanity are met on a day-to-day basis. In other words, through the human pursuit of vocations across the array of earthly stations the hungry are fed, the naked are clothed, the sick are healed, the ignorant are enlightened, and the weak are protected. That is, by working we actually participate in God's ongoing providence for the human race."[40] He took literally the biblical mandate, "Whether you eat or drink or whatever you do, do all to the glory of God."[41]

"Thus it was through his concept of work as a divine vocation that Luther cut through the two-tiered spirituality of the medieval world. No longer will the common laborer be shuffled off to the second class section of the Kingdom of God, while first class seats are reserved for those who ostensibly go beyond the call of duty and elect to take monastic vows as a form of special dedication to God."[42] It's not hard to see the implications of freedom and empowerment

---

40. Lee Hardy, *The Fabric of This World*, Grand Rapids, MI, Wm. B. Eerdmanns Publishing Company, 1990, p. 47.
41. I Cor. 10:31.
42. Ibid., p. 51.

for that person in the medieval world that was outside the monastic orders, but had to continue to plow, clean, hunt, cook, build, repair, feed, clothe, in other words, do what they were able, in order to bring wholeness and a better life for themselves *and others*. They now knew that they had worth in God's eyes, and that no matter what they worked at, God was pleased and society was better off for it.

JOHN CALVIN

As Luther redefined work in this way, he was having a major effect on the medieval concept of work, and in the process, prompting the thought life of his fellow reformers like John Calvin, of whom we have already spoken. His take on the medieval interpretation of the passage in Luke 10:38–42 of Jesus's visit with Martha and Mary is of pertinent interest here because he turned around what had been taught for several centuries to the Roman church. The passage became a lightning rod of sorts for interpreters like scholastic theologian Thomas Aquinas, who wanted to show that Jesus really was indicating for a life of contemplation over the life of action when He reminded Martha that she was worried and upset about many things but that only one thing was needed, and Mary had chosen what was better, i.e., sitting and listening to Jesus as He taught and talked.

This passage represented a prime biblical "proof text" for the contemplative life by the medieval interpreters; however, John Calvin could not travel with that take on the incident. "When we turn to Calvin's comments on this passage, what we find stands in stark contrast to the traditional interpretation. Refusing to assign an allegorical meaning to the persons of Mary and Martha, Calvin claims that Jesus was simply commending Mary's response to his presence over Martha's.

"Since Jesus was easily satisfied with modest accommodation, it was more important for Martha at that time to listen to what Jesus had to say than to make a big fuss about the food. But she was working too much, and had no time to hear his instruction. It was as if one were to give a magnificent reception to a prophet, and yet not to care about hearing him, but on the contrary, to make so great and unnecessary preparations, as to bury all the instruction. In commending Mary over Martha, Jesus was not commending a whole way of life over another—for certainly at times Mary also worked just as Martha also listened. Rather, he was addressing himself to the relative merits of their responses to his presence and message at that particular time. When he paid them a visit, one listened; the other did not. There is a time to work, and a time to listen. Jesus faulted Martha not for working in general, but for working at the wrong time."[43] In fact, in his examination of Calvin's works, Hardy makes the observation that "... Calvin took the notion that work as a purely secular matter to be a satanic deception."[44] Remember these words as we revisit Calvin's world in the next chapter.

These were amazing pronouncements by Luther and Calvin (and the other Reformers) about the place of Everyman in the social strata, not to mention God's own purposes for us, considering the medieval theological environment they came out of. We the workers were finally told that we were doing more than providing for the biological needs of the "true" spiritual persons of the Greek world. We were caring for the hungry, naked, and sick by doing what God has enabled us to do through our gifts and talents. That includes those of us who may feel we are grossly under used, perhaps as an assembly-line worker or ditch digger, and misunderstood to boot. There can be plenty of self-pity in those thoughts; however, God can look past that and assure us we have a special place in the work of the Kingdom, and we are a part of His plan to provide for the human race. What we are doing in that "station" in life is special to Him, and He is delighted with us and what we do. The problem is, we sometimes depend on others to speak those words of challenge and comfort that God wants to impart to us, as well as validation of what we do during the week. Where are those words most likely to come from if not church people and their leaders?

The Reformation was a time of liberation of God's people in many ways, and the insistence by the reformers that we are all priests, that God chose to continue His creative activity in this world

---

43. Lee Hardy, *The Fabric of This World*, Grand Rapids, MI, Wm. B. Eerdmanns Publishing Company, 1990, p. 55.

44. Ibid., p. 59, note 32.

through the work of human hands, that whatever work we do is not only special but necessary to provide for those in need was heady stuff for that day.

It is important to note that the Catholic Church itself has contributed to the understanding that work is an extension of creation in the wording of its official Catechism. It was produced in 1992 by a commission headed by Cardinal Joseph Ratzinger, who became Pope in 2005. Here is wording on human work from that document.

> *"Human work proceeds directly from persons created in the image of God and called to* prolong the work of creation *by subduing the earth both with and for one another." And, "In work, the person exercises and fulfills in part* the potential inscribed in his nature.*"*[45]

STUDY QUESTIONS

1. What did Abraham Kuyper mean by the terms "direct" or "mediate"?
2. What is the meaning of one of Luther's theological pillars, Solo Christo?
3. What is the name of the doctrine that forced a layer in between God, and you and me?
4. Why were sacramentalism and sacerdotalism so devastating to the spiritual life of the faithful?
5. What remnants of sacerdotalism remained in the Lutheran stream of Protestantism?
6. Ironically, both Martin Luther and the Catholic Church have made similar comments on the role of humans as "co-creators" or "to prolong the work of creation." How far apart in time were these comments?

---

45. *Catechism of the Catholic Church*, St. Paul, MN, The Wanderer Press, 1992, para. 2427, 2428.

Chapter Seven
Work During the Industrial Revolution

"Free productive activity is not only the activity by which we distinguish ourselves from the animals, but by it we can find true fulfillment as human beings"

Lee Hardy

We HAVE JUST COME THROUGH A description of the wonderful redefinition of work by the reformers of the sixteenth and seventeenth centuries, mainly by Luther and Calvin. Their "release" of work for Everyman and our attitude toward it reverberates to this day. Although their emphasis on the "universal priesthood" was a monumental theological accomplishment for the day, their overall mild stance against the existing ecclesiastical structure of the church did little to push back the dualism that had overwhelmed the church since the time of Constantine in the fourth century. Nevertheless, we will go forward with what we have, and see how man built on the foundation of the reformers' doctrines.

We are now addressing the history of the subject of Work from the seventeenth century on. This includes the work of the English reformers and the foundation they laid for the church in the New World, for we will eventually get to Puritanism, the so-called Protestant work ethic, and then even Marxism. It is a long road philosophically, but it took a relatively short time to make the transition—less than 350 years. This is a long time for those of us living in the twenty-first century, where immediacy is the rule of the day. However, considering the 1,200 years we languished with medieval thought between Constantine and Luther, this was a rapid evolution from the late Reformation to the Industrial Revolution at the beginning of the twentieth century. A lot of intellectual ground was covered, which has implications for us that lap at the very foundations of modern Western societies.

Although we have explored briefly Calvin's contributions to the release of work from the iron grip of medieval dualism during the Protestant Reformation, there is another aspect of his work that had a different effect on the thinking of believing Christians who heard Calvin teach about predestination. According to Max Weber,[46] Calvin's belief and teaching about predestination caused an emotional tension that colored the adherents' thinking away from the overwhelming grace of God and the salvation that is available to all who accept it. They became preoccupied with the demands of this new doctrine, which is as follows:

> *"By the decree of God, for the manifestation of His glory, some men and angels are predestinated unto everlasting life, and others fore-ordained to everlasting death. These angels and men, thus predestinated and fore-ordained, are particularly and unchangeably designed, and their number is so certain and definite, that it cannot be either increased or diminished."[47]*

That had the effect of putting people under enormous pressure to *know* whether they were in fact predestined to life or predestined to damnation. As Calvinism developed, a deep psychological need

---

46. Max Weber, *The Protestant Ethic and the Spirit of Capitalism*, Mineola, NY, Dover Publications, 2003.
47. Westminster Confession, 1647, Ch. III, para. 3, 4.

for clues about whether one was actually saved arose, and Calvinists looked to their success in worldly activity for those clues. Thus, they came to value profit and material success as signs of God's favor. One writer observes that believers in this system became "tensed up beings." Chesterton was less kind: "It would have been easy, in the Calvinistic seventeenth century, to fall into the bottomless pit of predestination."[48] Or as John Milton is often quoted on the subject of predestination, "Though I may be sent to hell for it, such a God will never command my respect." This is the same man who also said, "Give me the liberty to know, to utter, and to argue freely according to conscience, above all liberties." Man has the innate gift of and knowledge about his ability to know, utter, argue freely, create, and produce.

Among the nominally religious and early post-Protestants, people actually moved away from dependence on the sufficiency of Christ's work for salvation, much to the chagrin of other Protestants, especially Lutherans. During the Industrial Revolution, they invested work with more religious significance as a means of proving one's acceptance with God.[49] Modern-day Calvinists roundly criticize "the dreaded Weber thesis" as a theory only that doesn't deserve the prominent place in economic theory that it does in fact enjoy. This is understandable, as it places the teachings of Calvin in a negative light regarding God's endowment of free will on His created beings *to join Him in the beautiful process of co-creating by working, as Luther pointed out.*

Other religious groups, such as the Pietists, Methodists, and the Baptist sects, had similar attitudes to a lesser degree. Weber argues that this new attitude broke down the traditional economic system, paving the way for modern capitalism. However, once capitalism emerged as a major economic force, the Protestant values brought to bear on it seemed no longer necessary, for it had taken on a life of its own. Thus, the liberation of man from medieval dualism, which the reformers stood so solidly for, took an unexpected turn backward into the secularization of vocation and calling. In our day, we are

---

48. G. K. Chesterton, *Orthodoxy*, Wheaton, IL, Harold Shaw Publishers, 1994, p. 107.

49. R. Paul Stevens, *Doing God's Business*, Grand Rapids, MI, Wm. B. Eerdmans Publishing Company, 2006, p. 172.

locked into the spirit of capitalism because it is so useful for modern economic activity, and the church is nowhere to be seen.

As we stumbled toward the nineteenth and twentieth centuries, our theologians, on the one hand, had liberated us from medieval dualism, and then dragged us backward (unwittingly) to a more secular understanding of work and commercial activities and also a dimming of the grace of God that had been greatly clarified during the Reformation. As a result, we became vulnerable to the type of thinking we now know as Marxism. Whether we believe Max Weber had a place in the continuum of thinking that brought us to communism or not, there is no denying that the Protestant work ethic as he described it had a place in facilitating the capitalism that has dominated economic activity in the West from the eighteenth century onward. That this is so can be demonstrated by the differences in type and intensity of commercialism between Catholic and Protestant peoples, where Protestants have tended to be more aggressive. This has been shown by scholars such as Kuyper, who have analyzed these demographics as well as the effect religion has had on it.

The replacement of an ongoing belief in the saving and sufficient grace of God as a onetime expressed belief became a duty to continue in daily and secular activities so as to convince ourselves that we were one of the elect that God had already chosen beforehand. The Lutheran idea of "stations" in life, vocations, and calling was lost in the mist of just having to "do something." It was very hard to believe, in the late nineteenth century, that God had a very special thing He had equipped us to do, when the enormous frenzy of secular capitalism was flexing its muscles and the great capitalists of that time were conscripting millions into its mines and factories to dig and make, in greater and greater quantities. Those of us working at that time were easy targets for someone to articulate our sour thoughts on it all. That person was Karl Marx, the so-called "philosopher of labor."

In many ways, Marx was ahead of the church in realizing that a major part of the human psyche was our ability to engage in free productive activity, step back and realize what we had done, and then choose our future activities from that base. This was done by an exercise of *free will*. As Lee Hardy puts it, "*Free* productive activity is not only the activity by which we distinguish ourselves from the animals, but by it we can find true fulfillment as human beings. Ultimate satisfaction is found in surveying the *freely created works of our own hands* (italics mine)."[50]

It's a long road from there to the stifling mass production lines of the early twentieth century. However, knowing that Marx had correctly identified one of the central characteristics of us as created beings, that being to engage in free productive activity, it became a short road for those naturally created free human beings to become "alienated labor," as Marx describes them. "Since modern workers have been denied fulfillment in the potentially human activity of production, they will seek fulfillment in the typically animal activities of eating, drinking and procreating, or at most also in his dwelling and in personal adornment. Under the aegis of capitalism, work has been made so disagreeable it is avoided like the plague"[51]

So now we not only had a sacred/secular division, but the specter of those in the capitalistic portion of the secular commercial realm also caused a further downgrading of the natural creative productive human self that all peoples want, to an almost animalistic condition. In some ways, working under those conditions was no better than being a laborer in a guild in the Dark Ages. In both cases the workers were locked into a situation that was very hard to break out of.

We now know that communism ran its course in Eastern Europe in a mere 70 years and that the countries that had absorbed this ideology were vastly far behind in the freedom and prosperity enjoyed by the peoples in countries operating under a system of free enterprise. Marx went too far and envisioned humans becoming almost God-like in their breaking out of being alienated labor. However, he had correctly identified a basic human need for free production, a characteristic that God Himself had put there.

It's worth noting that a system that capitalizes on the human potential for free production is vastly more generous in providing for the needs of the citizenry, as well as generating surplus assets

---

50. Lee Hardy, *The Fabric of This World*, Grand Rapids, MI, Wm. B. Eerdmanns Publishing Company, 1990, p. 30.
51. Karl Marx, *Essential Writings*.

that are available to those in need. A discussion like this can become politically charged, even in our day in the West, but for our purposes, we may say that the opportunity for plying a trade or occupation for which we are suited and gifted is more freely available outside a managed commercial society such as communism or socialism.

No discussion of Work in the context of alienated labor would be complete without considering many of our own jobs that contain more tedium than we ever thought possible. Who among us hasn't wondered why we have to slog through so many menial tasks, maybe every day. You could say that most of us suffer through jobs that are at least partially noncreative. Yes, and the sky is blue. It's a fallen world and we're in it, and "nobody knows the trouble I've seen," as the song goes. That's not to make light of anyone's situation.

True enough, we may have an assembly-line job, or what others might say is menial. Let me encourage you, friend, to believe that there is no place on earth where God cannot use you to be a light in the dark. Brother Lawrence did so while he was washing dishes in the monastery kitchen, and he became a huge light for many generations because of his attitude. We may not be in the job of our dreams, but what if God has called you to be where you are right now. Someone may need to know you and hear from you. A short test is to ask God to bless you and put you in the most productive place for His Kingdom. Pray that prayer regularly for a month and see what God will do. Jabez did that, and God heard. See I Chronicles 4:9–10 for the short account of his life, and for the prayer that thousands pray every day. This is not just some serendipity thing we do. It's a serious attempt to be and do what God wants so very much for you in your work.

STUDY QUESTIONS

1. What can we do to find fulfillment as human beings?
2. What did Max Weber teach about Calvinism?
3. What major human need did Karl Marx identify?
4. What Old Testament prayer can be helpful in asking God to put us in the most productive place for His Kingdom?

Part Two
The Future of Work

Chapter Eight
The Modern Church Wakes Up

"What the church should be telling (the carpenter) is this:
that the very first demand that his religion makes upon him is
that he should make good tables."

Dorothy Sayers

Aₛ ᴏᴜʀ ᴀɴᴄᴇꜱᴛᴏʀꜱ ʟᴀʙᴏʀᴇᴅ 100 ʏᴇᴀʀꜱ ago in the West, the church was blissfully unaware that there was a major disconnect between what God had set out in the Bible regarding work and what was being observed every day in the lives of its people. It seems incredible now that the church contented itself with just ministering to the needs of its downtrodden workers rather than also inquiring into the philosophical differences between God's desires and what was actually happening.

The truth is, we were living in an era of drought in that thinking that had lasted 1,900 years and virtually the entire history of the world from the time of the Flood up to Christ. Only in the time of Christ had the worldly understanding of a dualistic attitude toward work and people been reversed. It had been reversed back again so quickly by the church itself from the fourth century on that it's understandable that in the throes of the Industrial Age we couldn't see the forest for the trees. But rather than being judgmental about it, it will be more productive for us to recount what I call a "Great Awakening" to the marketplace by the modern church. An awakening is, in fact, taking place now, and there are many of God's finest, laboring to articulate what is happening and why. We will point out who began the inquiry and how work took on a whole new meaning or, shall we say more accurately, began to recover the meaning God intended for it in the first place.

In the middle part of the twentieth century, a British Catholic lady named Dorothy Sayers began making some bold statements about what the church should be doing and saying about those of us who work in the marketplace. Here is a sample:

> *"The church's approach to an intelligent carpenter is usually confined to exhorting him not to be drunk and disorderly in his leisure hours, and to come to church on Sundays. What the church should be telling him is this: that the very first demand that his religion makes upon him is that he should make good tables."*[52]

That was astounding rhetoric considering the age in which she was writing. There had been very little coming from the church on the subject of work and vocations in the previous 400 years, before she had effectively and suddenly opened the debate on what we now called "marketplace ministry." It's a weak term, in my view, so we will use "The Call to Work." The truth is that Ms. Sayers called the church to stop thinking about itself so much and have a look at that 95 percent of the life its parishioners spend outside the walls and maybe even be involved in it.

Thinking about that place outside the walls would be pleasing to God, for Jesus Christ did not teach and disciple His followers from inside the synagogues and temples. He was on the dusty trails

---

52. Dorothy Sayers, *Creed or Chaos*, Manchester, NH, Sophia Institute Press, 1974, p. 106.

with His men. He spent time *in their homes* and riding *in their boats.* He impacted their work life, for He knew the value of showing His power *where they lived and breathed.* The storm waters were calmed; they pulled up 153 fish where there were none before. He discussed morals with tax collectors *in their homes.*

The demoniacs didn't make it to church, so He went to the tombs and cast the demons out of them there. In the very first major dissertation by our Lord in the Sermon on the Mount, He mentions not one thing about how we are to spend time in the synagogue or temple designing or funding the new addition or the next evangelism program. It all has to do with our thoughts and behavior as we live our lives *outside* those places and He was with us there.

As if a dam had burst, the next 60 years produced a plethora of scholars, authors, and speakers who held forth on the subject of the sacred/secular division, especially in the church itself. It began to dawn on theologians and teachers that first, there is a philosophical problem here and second, there is no good theological basis for going forward. The church had been concentrating on itself for so long that it had no theological link from the bible to the workplace. There was no link from inside the church to the outside. Sayers herself indicates that "If man's fulfillment of his nature is to be found in *the full expression of his divine creativeness,* then we urgently need a Christian doctrine of work, which shall provide not only for proper conditions of employment, but also that the work shall be such as a man may do with his whole heart, *and that he shall do it for the very work's sake.*"[53] This is a very important point, and one that virtually all modern (especially theological) writers pass over.

There is a cornucopia of books written by Christians on subjects ranging from finding help on how to sell, how to be successful in business, the challenge of fusing Christian and business values, and so forth. Very seldom does the thought occur to us and our theologians that God has deliberately designed mankind to do the work of commerce, including agriculture, teaching, medicine, law, government, entertainment, manufacturing, and buying and selling. In

---

53. Ibid., p. 71.

other words, He equipped us for those types of tasks and is especially happy when we acknowledge His hand in our workday and that He equipped us to do that secular work. We, in the course of our workday, are the missionaries and disciples in the process of doing our work. A few years later, Christian Smith noted: "A graceful spirituality of everyday life is not the dominant spirituality in Christian circles today. There are many questions and issues to be worked out in theory and practice. Nevertheless such *a spirituality of everyday life* begs to be cultivated and brought to maturity as we seek to go to the root and find renewal."[54] Many authors took up the challenge of articulating that theology, and the discussion is beginning to take place.

Here is a sampling of thought by several authors on this subject. Please note the common thread of condemnation of the dualism we have discussed and fought for several millennia. We will then discuss what work is not:

> *"Work is not primarily a thing one does to live, but the thing one lives to do. It is, or it should be, the full expression of the worker's faculties, the thing in which he finds spiritual, mental, and bodily satisfaction, and* the medium in which he offers himself to God. *Every man should do the work for which he is fitted by nature. It is the business of the Church to recognize that the secular vocation, as such, is sacred. Christian people, and particularly perhaps the Christian clergy, must get it firmly into their heads that when a man or woman is called to a particular job of secular work that is as true a vocation as though he or she were called to specifically religious work.*
>
> *"In nothing has the Church so lost her hold on reality as in her failure to understand and respect the secular vocation. She has allowed work and religion to become separate departments, and is astonished to find that, as a result, the secular work of the world is turned to purely selfish and destructive ends, and that the greater part of the world's intelligent workers have become irreligious, or at least, uninterested in religion. But is it*

---

54. Christian Smith, *Going to the Root*, Scottdale, PA, Herald Press, 1992, p. 121.

astonishing? How can anyone remain interested in a religion which seems to have no concern with nine-tenths of his life? Let the church remember this: that every maker and worker is called to serve God in his profession or trade, not outside it. *The official Church wastes time and energy, and moreover, commits sacrilege, in demanding that secular workers would neglect their proper vocation in order to do Christian work— by which she means ecclesiastical work."*[55]

"One of the greatest hindrances to the Christian's internal peace is the common habit of dividing our lives into two areas— the sacred and the secular. But this state of affairs is wholly unnecessary. As these areas are conceived to exist apart from each other and to be morally and spiritually incompatible, and as we are compelled by the necessities of living to be always crossing back and forth from the one to the other, our inner lives tend to break up so that we live a divided instead of a unified life. . . . I believe this state of affairs to be wholly unnecessary. We have gotten ourselves on the horns of a dilemma, true enough, but the dilemma is not real. It is a creature of misunderstanding. The sacred-secular antithesis has no foundation in the New Testament."[56]

"How does fear of man become campaigning weather for dragging souls into hell? The answer will sound almost heretical: It keeps the person from experiencing something God created in order that he might seek after Him—pleasure. The peculiar pleasure I mean is the one 1924 Olympic medalist Eric Liddell noted in Chariots of Fire: *'God also made me fast, and when I run, I feel His pleasure.' It is the pleasure of the Reformation rediscovered in Romans 12, the happy convergence of what we're good at and what builds God's kingdom. No longer must I be a baker or a smith just because daddy and granddaddy were bakers or smiths. No longer are some professions holier*

55. Dorothy Sayers, *Creed or Chaos*, Manchester, NH, Sophia Institute Press, 1974, pp. 101–108.

56. A. W. Tozer, *The Pursuit of God*, Camp Hill, PA, Christian Publications, 1993, pp. 109, 111.

than others. All helpful work is sacred if done unto God *(I Thessalonians 4:11).*"[57]

"Living a meaningful life consists simply in embracing the responsibilities and work given to us, whatever they are. The nature of work itself connects us with the moral order. . . . The workbench, the kitchen counter, the computer station, or any other workspace is an altar. There is intrinsic meaning to work well done—*and when we fail to grasp this, we become hollow persons.*"[58]

"No one in our world can work at a job of that sort as Dwarfs and Talking Moles work in Narnia; but then, of course, Moles and Dwarfs don't look on it as work. They like digging."[59]

This amazing compilation is just a sampling of those modern writers who have held forth on the subject of work as the church should be seeing it, and as we workers should be seeing it. It is also a drop on the thirsty tongue for the rest of us who slog away at our "jobs" with no real encouragement from the church that we are doing God's will in our work. Make no mistake: The fault is not only with the church and its teachings. We are where the buck stops for our own actions. We must be doing the right thing with our gifts and calling, and we must teach our children the same.

Note that the right attitude on this major portion of our lives can enhance our inner peace, as Tozer points out; help us be happier, as C. S. Lewis's talking moles were; create spiritual, mental, and bodily satisfaction, as Sayers points out; and provide just plain pleasure, as Seu points out. This is a pretty good list of good things! Without a correct understanding of our work and why we do it, all these things can be denied us. We can be distraught in our inner being, spend a large part of our day without being satisfied, and not have the happy pleasure of knowing we are doing God's will by doing our work well, whatever that is.

---

57. Andree Seu, "Doing What You Love," *World Magazine*, June 14–21, 2008, p. 87.

58. Chuck Colson, *The Good Life*, Carol Stream, IL, Tyndale House, 2005, p. 89.

59. C. S. Lewis, *The Silver Chair*, New York, Macmillan, 1970, p. 198.

All this can seem quite out of reach for the average person like you and me, but it is not, if we are working "as unto the Lord" and doing what He has equipped us to do. God wants to help us be there. Start by recognizing the definition of what full, creative, Godly work is not:

1. *Earning money to support the family.* Of course, it's good and necessary; in fact, it is God's command that we do just that, but it's not the only reason. If we are intentional about pursuing God's best intentions for our work life, will He not supply our material needs by doing it?

2. *Earning money to spend on pleasure.* That's not a bad thing, but lack of satisfaction in our work can send us fleeing to pleasure, à la the TGIF mentality.

3. *Earning money to tithe and support ministries and help the needy.* Of course, it is that, too, but not the main reason. The Lord does expect us to give back in money and time to those in need. That's one of the universal calls we must all answer. However, this, too, will be added in by God as we intentionally pursue His best for us.

4. *Using the workplace as a mission opportunity.* Of course it is—and thank God for the opportunities to appropriately witness in your workplace—but it is not the only reason we are there. If you disconnect here, reconsider what it is that you are equipped for and called to do. If you can't picture yourself doing that in the marketplace, reconsider what God said about it in Chapter One. We are here to co-create with God. The witnessing opportunities *will* come.

Let's go over this again. What is work then, and what is it for? It is the reason God created us—to work alongside Him and co-create with Him. The Fall stunted that but didn't eliminate it, for the full resources of heaven are available to those who believe in God's power to in-fill everything we do. We are made to work and to work productively, as even Karl Marx knew. What's it for? To glorify God in the everyday things He gives us to do. It gives God pleasure to see us working with all the gifts and resources He gave to us. Eric Liddell knew and felt God's pleasure when he ran fast, because he knew it was God's gift to him to do so.

There is another very important subject to address at this point. There is a large segment of the working public that isn't exercising their professional training but working hard, nevertheless, in a job where the rewards are great and the training minimal to nonexistent. They are the mothers of this world who may have a career but choose to stay with their children to raise, nurture, and train them with love and care as no one else can. Care can be purchased, in the form of a nanny or day care of some sort, but none can do it like the mother.

We have spoken aggressively about our mandate to co-create with God. This would be true of parents also, especially the mother at home as she is exercising the instructions to parents in Proverbs: "Train up a child in the way he should go, even when he is old he will not depart from it."[60] If a child is incomplete, it would be in two areas: one, his relationship with God; the other, his exercise of his unique gifting in society, usually in a secular setting. Not surprisingly, the church speaks only of the first. Parents play a major role in identifying and encouraging the child's special gifts. Every child has that unique package, and the church should be helping here, too.

What training can and should there be for the role of parenting? A mother is hardwired for this job. Who can teach her to make sure she gets up in the night to care for her child's needs? Yes, fathers do this, too, but it is the mother who has all the instincts to do it and to love that child as no one else on earth. She is held up as the standard for tender, loving care. "But we proved to be gentle among you, as a nursing mother cares for her own children."[61]

We should also note that there are many Universal Calls that exempt no one. No matter our profession or training or station or circumstance, we must all obey the commands of our Lord to conduct ourselves rightly in every aspect of life. We have a list in Appendix B, and you may want to add some of your own.

---

60. Prov. 22:6.
61. I Thess. 2:7.

I can almost hear you now: "That's all very nice, but how does the doctrine of Work apply to me?" Don't feel badly about asking the question, because I did and that's what set me on the path to find the solid ground on which I could serve God in the marketplace. What's in it for you is a greater sense of fulfillment and satisfaction than you've ever had in doing your thoroughly secular work.

A word needs to be said about so many of us who may be laboring in jobs where it's hard to see anything special about what we do or how it may be impacting the Kingdom. It can be said with great assurance that no human that ever lived has filled God's best for him or her in a perfect way. We all go downhill from there. However, don't allow yourself a pity party here. You may even be a professional clergy type that has never felt comfortable filling that role with your own giftings as they unfolded. So what? We are so conditioned in our dualistic thinking that for you to go to a secular calling would be to go backwards. Not so. Go do what the Lord has equipped you to do. Be free!

All of our careers and work life need to be tweaked from time to time. Don't allow yourself to moan that "nobody knows the trouble I've seen." There have been times in my own career that more patience with my current situation would have been a virtue. Nevertheless, God wants to help, guide, lead, equip, and fill with enthusiasm for the ways we exercise our command to work. He is all about walking with us every day in things large and small. Test Him by asking very simply, "What would You have me do differently today?"

The solid ground, by the way, is not really in the marketplace. It's in your heart that knows God made you to be doing what He's equipped you to do. When that happens, you will know that God is sending His Holy Spirit to work alongside you, and yes, you will see miracles happen through you. The corollary, and we don't mean to trivialize it with that term, is that the Kingdom of God will expand at a rate we have known nothing about until now. As we workers find our place, work hard as unto the Lord, and glorify Him in the process, good things will always happen in us and those around us. There was a saying passed around in the church a few years ago. "When the sheep are healthy, they reproduce quite naturally." I long to see a healthy church where the sheep (us) are nurtured, equipped, and encouraged. When that happens, we will multiply the Kingdom quite naturally—no evangelism program needed.

STUDY QUESTIONS

1. What is the significance of Jesus Christ engaging in His ministry in the everyday work life of His followers?
2. What prevented the church from constructing a theological link from the Bible to the workplace?
3. What is the difference between marketplace ministry and "The Call to Work"?
4. What does Andree Seu mean when she says Romans 12 is "the happy convergence of what we're good at and what builds God's Kingdom"?

Chapter Nine
The Call

"Here I am, send me!"

Isa. 6:8

As I wrestled with what my personal "call" might be, I understood that I was dealing with a pretty auspicious term. After all, wasn't that reserved for the clergy, the "called and ordained servants of the Word"? But wait, that's the whole point of this book—the fact that we all can and do have a call. It's no small thing, and likewise not easily understood by twenty-first-century man. So let's try to sort this out before coming to our "what to do now" chapter. What, Lord, is my purpose in life?

No less a wordsmith than Os Guinness has written a 300-page book, *The Call*, on this very subject, in which he tries valiantly (and effectively) to approach and answer every question a person might have about their unique position in God's economy.

Paulo Coelho wrote one of the most popular novels of the twentieth century, *The Alchemist*, which basically deals with Santiago's search for his purpose in life, what he calls his Personal Legend. The book was devoured by presidents, Hollywood stars, and 22 million others!

Rick Warren is one of the most prolific author/pastors of our time. The most famous of his works is on the subject of—you guessed it—*The Purpose Driven Life*. It has been read, passed around, and discussed in small groups across the land.

Why are these books so popular? These are just a few of the many books that have addressed this specific question: "What is my call if, in fact, I have one at all?" There is something in our very souls that demands to know, for we fear that if we don't have that call or purpose, our hoped-for life of meaning just went in the tank. As an extreme example, why would a person take their own life? It is often a case of perceived hopelessness, or a life that did have promise and was squandered.

There are several good synonyms for the word "call" as we are using it. How about "purpose," or "personal legend," or "giftedness," or "personal responsibility," or even "co-creator"? However we choose to identify it, there is obviously a great hunger in every soul to know we are special, we are gifted to do *something*, and that someone cares.

Let's try to break this down into digestible bites:

Stations—This is a term the Reformers used to describe the functions we each fill, such as father, mother, and provider. These are usually not unique to an individual, but it's helpful to recognize that we do fit into a pattern to which God and society at large can positively react.

Vocations—This was also used first by the Reformers to refer to a specific set of skills for which we were trained. Parenthetically, some will be better carpenters than others, even though the same training was received. This may be a first inkling of a unique skill set we as individuals have.

Gifting—This starts to identify more closely with us as individuals but perhaps still doesn't show the whole picture about ourselves. For example, I may be gifted as a precise person. Does that make me a mathematician, cabinet maker, machinist, or accountant? They all are precise people, but other "gifts" are added to my personal toolbox to come closer to what I am. It's not hard to see that the many thousands of individual skills and gifts can be combined in so many billions of ways that no one who has ever lived will be like me.

Call—This category gets very specific to me as a person. A call can be an audible voice from God, experienced by very few, or a tug in my heart that drew me to engineering, or you into medicine, or accounting, or assembling autos. I just knew I wanted to go there. It is based on my specific set of physical gifts and temperament and is unique to me, and will be something I like to do.

Was it a call of God that caused and equipped me to sell parts for railroads? Perhaps, or was it a natural progression of a life of commerce that led me there from the original call of engineering? There may not be a last and final answer for many of us, but the important thing for me was and is to recognize God's hand in that equipping process and the ongoing progression of my career. It's a wonderful thing for us to recognize God's hand in it, and He is pleased for us to do so.

It's appropriate to address a mild form of dualism that exists in our time. It says that yes, pursue what you believe God equipped you to do, but in order to really be doing God's will, your calling must include regular and purposeful interaction with people. "Merely" working with your hands as an artist, craftsman, machinist, assembly-line worker, or alone as a lab tech, scientist, or whatever is good but not the best.

Unless we are total hermits without any relationships at all, we can all fulfill the Great Commission in our work—to make disciples of all nations wherever we are and in whatever we're doing. This is by simply being deliberate about moving anyone we meet along the line of understanding about the Savior and who He is. Because our work and calling are all different, we will meet different people that other Christians may never see. No, we can't be adding layers onto the words of Christ that aren't there. He paid the price to destroy them all, and we are all equipped to serve Him in our own unique way.

Those that did include Michelangelo, who lay alone on his back on scaffolding for weeks at a time, painting in plaster (fresco) one of the most beautiful and sublime depictions of Creation ever, on the

Sistine Chapel ceiling, or Leonardo DaVinci, who painted the Last Supper, a work that has ministered to centuries of believers. Isaac Newton and Albert Einstein, each in his own generation, worked for the most part alone to unlock mysteries of science that blew open many new chapters in our understanding of the majesty of God. (And each of these gave Him credit for their discoveries.) How about Rembrandt, notorious for being not particularly good with people, who painted, among other things, one of the most insightful and stunning depictions of the Prodigal Son ever done. It has been studied over and over by theologians trying to plumb its depths. See Henri Nouwen's book, *The Prodigal*, for a sample.

No matter where you are in being able to do what you've always wanted to do, or equipped to do, there is value in thanking God for your current circumstance and asking to be used more than you could ask or think. God is not put off by such a prayer; in fact, He wants us to think bigger. Who among us has ever been called specifically by an act of God to do the next thing? Some, but not many. However, many of God's people can testify to a point-to-point guidance by Him along the path of our careers. I am one of those.

A handful of biblical characters, like Abraham, who heard God call him from Mesopotamia, Moses at the burning bush, and Paul on the road to Damascus, were those who had that rare experience of a direct encounter with God. However, don't lose sight of the fact that they all could have said no. How many of us have said no, when we were unwittingly staring His call in the face through circumstances only we understood. We have the gift of free will to say no, and most of us, sadly, have exercised that gift. A frequent prayer I have about myself is that I would always have ears to hear when God is speaking to me. That, I have come to see, is *not* a rare experience for those who call on Him. God does speak, and He will give us ears to hear.

What we don't have is the privilege to say to God that He has put us in the wrong place in life, or equipped us in the wrong way, or even has not equipped us with anything useful at all. That would show a lack of trust on our part. How many times could Joseph have said that, starting with being thrown in a pit by his eleven brothers? Not fair. Not a great start on a great adventure to eventually save his family from starvation! In his case the end result was many years down the road, a road that went through two prison terms in a foreign land, and he had no foreknowledge of the end game.

I encourage you to draw God into your deliberations on what your gifting and calling are, and what you are to do about them next—if not for all time, at least for what is next. The psalmist says God's Word is a lamp for our feet, not for the entire path at once. God does want to guide and direct. He is there, and He is not silent. Go for it.

STUDY QUESTIONS

1. What's behind the drive of people to know the purpose for their life?
2. How is a vocation different from a call?
3. Are some forms of secular work more valuable than others?

Chapter Ten
The New Church

"And He gave some as apostles, and some as prophets,
and some as evangelists, and some as pastors and teachers,
for the equipping of the saints for the work of service."

Eph. 4:11

I$_F$ YOU AND I ARE STILL together so far, what are the chances that your church will have the slightest clue what you are talking about when you approach them about a new vision you have for yourself, and your new understanding of the church's responsibility toward its people who work in a secular setting? Here are the thoughts of a person in a similar situation:

"In the almost 30 years of my professional career, my church has never once suggested that there be any type of accounting of my on-the-job ministry to others. My church has never once offered to improve those skills which could make me a better minister, nor has it ever asked if I needed any kind of support in what I was doing. There has never been an enquiry into the types of ethical decisions I must face, or whether I seek to communicate the faith to my co-workers. I have never been in a congregation

where there was any type of public affirmation of a ministry in my career. In short, I must conclude that my church doesn't have the least interest whether or how I minister in my daily work."[62]

Those are pretty direct, even harsh words by a long-time businessman and presumably commit-ed Christian and member of a local church body. Perhaps your experience is not like that, and your pastor has taken a great interest in what you do during the week and how you walk that out from a Kingdom perspective, and encourages you in your secular calling. However, if that quote *does* describe your experience, you are like the vast majority of us, that 99 percent of the church population that is not on the church staff. There are two points to be made from this little example. One involves personal growth; the other, the corporate community of believers.

PERSONAL GROWTH

I will use my own example of what happened when I first apprehended the principle of co-creating with God in my work, and when I realized He had equipped me for doing that and was pleased about it. I became energized by my secular job, and was free to put my heart and soul into the work because I knew He was pleased with what I was doing with those locomotive parts I have fussed about for most of my career. I became more creative and productive, and more people came to know the God I serve. I began discipling men who asked for that to happen. I had no desire to retire, and had a joy in the journey of my work.

What matters is that God is in our work, and wants you and your family to have a prosperous heart about serving Him. In many ways, the ball is then in God's court. He is interested that you serve Him in the fullest way possible and according to your gifting and perhaps even calling, for you are no longer your own. It bears repeating that

---

62. W. Diehl, *Christianity and Real Life*, pp. v–vi, as quoted by R. Paul Stevens, *The Other Six Days*, Grand Rapids, MI, Wm. B. Eerdmanns Publishing Company, 1999, p. 49.

we are ultimately responsible for finding out God's vision for our own lives, and then carrying it out.

We cannot lay all of this at the feet of the church. There is a parable at the end of the Sermon on the Mount that is sometimes misinterpreted, even by Bible teachers. It says basically that if we act on His commands, our house will be on a rock. If we hear the commands and don't follow them, our house is on sand. The lesson is as simple as that. We are the ones to take action to rise up and believe God has a unique purpose and set of gifts for us.

I am amazed and saddened by the number of people who denigrate themselves and their gifting, and allow themselves to be downtrodden by the environment in which they work. For example, secular societies regularly look down on the young parents who are working valiantly to raise their own children, as we have already discussed. Let me ask you: What effect do those comments have on the eternal worth of the jobs these people are doing, in the eyes of God? If you said "Nothing!" you would be right. Another large group of people who are trying their level best to exercise their considerable gifts on behalf of our children, most of the time with little respect, indifference, and sometimes downright hostility, would be the nation's teachers. Here is another question: What is the eternal worth of the effort today's teachers are making on behalf of our children, in spite of the attitude of us parents? If you said, "A lot!" you would be right.

Here, then, is the truth that sets us free to work creatively in our secular settings: God is the one we are pleasing. *He is the One* who equipped us. *He is the One* who delights the most in what you are doing. *He is the One* who wants you to keep doing what you're doing. *He is the One* who gives you a peace and a joy and unexplainable creativity in the doing of your work. *He is the One* who makes you wise in the long-range vision you have for your work as well as in the day-to-day tasks. Listen to the words of a contemporary pastor who "gets" that connection between wisdom and the creativity God gave us to do our work:

> *"Wisdom and creativity are related subjects in the Bible. In fact, creativity is a manifestation of wisdom in the context of*

excellence and integrity. Wisdom is personified in Proverbs 8, and is the companion of God at the creation of all things. Therefore wisdom and creativity must not be separated in the mind of the believer. They are the essential tools needed to complete our assignment of being an effective witness to the lost. It is wisdom that makes our role in this world desirable to them. While most Christians have a value for wisdom, most do not have an equal value for the role of creativity in their God-given responsibilities. Yet it is creativity that illustrates the presence of wisdom: "Wisdom is vindicated by all her children." *Luke 7:35*[63]

We don't have space to list all the different vocations, stations, callings, sets of gifting, professions, and just plain jobs we all have that might deserve special attention. However, there are some things we can all do individually to begin apprehending what God's intent is for us in our work. Here are some suggestions:

1. Thank God for the *unique gifting* you have, knowing that no one else can do what you do, and that He is delighted with you.
2. Pray about what *God's best* is for you in your daily work.
3. If you are starting your work life or the education process leading up to that, seek the counsel of family, friends, and/or church to help you discern the right path.
4. Start moving. There is value in tarrying for God's answer to your prayers, but the danger is waiting for Him to do everything for you. Just do it!
5. Make an inventory of your own interests, perhaps including some you have always wanted to do but never could. It doesn't matter whether you see that it is possible or not. Our spiritual vision can be very dim at times, and God is not limited by that.
6. Stay focused on the non-negotiables of behavior.

But there is still this little matter of the church itself.

---

63. Bill Johnson, *A Life of Miracles*, Day 259, Shippensburg, PA, Destiny House Publishers, 2008.

THE COMMUNITY OF BELIEVERS

Modern church leaders love to talk about being "missional" and "relevant," "solid or liquid," and so on. What that all means can be a mystery to those of us who serve in a secular setting, especially since the church's definition of "relevant" has nothing to do with what I do during the week. Much energy is given to discipleship programs, evangelism, and outreach. Those are not bad things, but all are conceived to happen from within the walls of the church.

What we are talking about, however, is God-appointed and -anointed work that can do all of that with one stroke. When we are encouraged and empowered, all of the programs that come from within the church happen very naturally, and in our own secular settings where the fish are pulled out of the water.

Here is a pivot point for how the church can think. When regular folks like you and me can be empowered in our secular settings to really believe we are serving God the way *He likes it and created us for,* something happens to our spirit. We come to see we are special, and that the work we do is pleasing to God. The man quoted at the beginning of the chapter may know that about himself, but he is puzzled as to why the church doesn't know it. We see that God wouldn't have it any other way, and that as He equips us in miraculous ways to do that job, things happen in our soul.

The church can be forgiven for not totally embracing what we have said, and the enthusiasm we have about a new outlook. However, it does have an obligation to inquire into the fullness of God's vision for this day, regardless of where it leads. Its track record in being able to do that is not spectacular, shall we say. For example, a large part of the church dismissed the worldwide outpouring of the Spirit in the twentieth century, and thereby missed a major move of God that is still going and comprises the fastest growing segment of the church on earth. Also, many have been drawn in by the large reservoir of money staring them in the face in America and have lost Kingdom focus and personal integrity.

We have also seen various manifestos, universal creeds, and declarations over the last 50 years in a sincere attempt to unite the church, without a single nod to the calling of you and me in the workplace. It is my conviction that the church has missed a major move of God by not acknowledging and acting on the many voices being raised from within the church, about working for God in secular professions.

OK, then, let's design a new church to equip and empower its people! If we were to do that, what would it look like?

1. First, it would remind everyone that there are some non-negotiables for the behavior of everyone. These come out of the mouth of our Lord. He commanded us to exercise compassion to clothe the naked, feed the hungry, lift up the downtrodden, and visit them in prison. Also see that list of Universal Calls in Appendix B we have referred to.

2. Second, it would remind us that all of our relationships, whether on the job, in the market, or at home, should be filtered through the template of discipleship. His parting command on the Mount of Ascension was that we make disciples of all nations.

3. Third, the church would be involved in helping you and your family find the right fit for your gifting. That could happen through the Pastor, the Board of Elders, the new Equipping Task Force, your Home Group leader, or a good friend.

4. The church, whether Home Church or Mega church, would follow up with you on a career search, career change, aptitude testing, and accountability. This is especially appropriate with young people, and it wouldn't be too soon to start the process with grade schoolers, just to pray with them and prime the pump with suggestions.

5. The church would make sure you are doing all you can to support and raise your family. Not doing that makes you worse than an infidel.[64] You don't want to be one of those!

6. Someone from the Equipping Task Force would visit you at your workplace, maybe annually, to encourage you and pray with you where appropriate.

---

64. I Tim. 5:8.

7. The church would conduct regular instruction on this new paradigm on what God thinks about work, what it means to serve the Lord fully according to His gifting and call, and your expectation for Him to be your creation-leader in the workplace.

8. The church would have a consecration service for all those serving the Lord in non-church staff situations. There could be anointing and laying on of hands. Perhaps the Lord would deliver a Word of Knowledge or Word of Wisdom for each person on how to better focus on His purposes in the workplace.

Let's get to work!

STUDY QUESTIONS

1. How does your pastor or priest involve himself in your secular occupation/call?
2. Who is ultimately responsible for finding God's vision for our lives?
3. What is the eternal truth that sets us free to work productively and creatively?
4. Discuss the six things we can do to apprehend what God's intent is for us in our work.
5. Discuss some aspects of a church specifically designed to equip and empower it's people for their secular work.

Appendices

The Call to Work

Appendix A
Major Religions & Philosophies

Date	Name	Common Name	Country	Religion
1850 BC	Abram	Abraham	Ur	Judaism
1400 BC	Vedda Peoples	Hindu	India	Hinduism
800 BC	Upanishad Peoples	Hindu	India	Hinduism
628–551 BC	Zarathustra of Balkh	Zoroaster	Persia	Zoroastrianism
563–483 BC	Siddhartha Gautama	Buddha	India	Buddhism
551–479 BC	Kong Fuzi	Confucius	China	Confucianism
550 BC	Lao-Tsu	Lao-Tsu	China	The Tao
470–399 BC	Socrates	Socrates	Greece	Philosophy
428–348 BC	Plato	Plato	Greece	Philosophy
384–322 BC	Aristotle	Aristotle	Greece	Philosophy
4 BC–AD 29	Jesus Christ	Jesus	Palestine	Christianity
AD 354–430	Augustine of Hippo	Augustine	Algeria	Catholicism
AD 570–632	Muhammad	Muhammad	Arabia	Islam
AD 1483–1546	Martin Luther	Luther	Germany	Protestantism

Appendix B
Universal Calls

WALK WORTHY

"I therefore a prisoner for the Lord, urge you to walk in a manner worthy of the calling to which you have been called, with all humility and gentleness, with patience, bearing with one another in love."

Eph. 4:1, 2

LOVE AND SERVE ONE ANOTHER

"For God is not unjust so as to overlook your work and the love you have shown for His name in serving the saints, as you still do."

Heb. 6:10

SHOW INTEGRITY

"Then Daniel answered and said before the king, 'Let your gifts be for yourself, and give your rewards to another. Nevertheless, I will read the writing to the king and make known to him the interpretation."

Dan. 5:17

WITNESS TO THE FAITH

"But concerning brotherly love you have no need that I should write to you, for you yourselves are taught by God to love one another; and indeed you do so toward all the brethren who are in all Macedonia. But we urge you brethren, that you increase more and more; that you also aspire to lead a quiet life, to mind your own business, and to work with your own hands, as we commanded you."

I Thess. 4:9–11

FAMILY RESPONSIBILITIES

"But if anyone does not provide for his own, and especially for those of his household, he has denied the faith and is worse than an unbeliever."

I Tim. 5:8

GLORIFY GOD

"Therefore, whether you eat or drink, or whatever you do, do all to the glory of God."

I Cor. 10:31

Appendix C
Suggested Reading

Barnette, Henlee H., *Christian Calling and Vocation*, Grand Rapids, MI, Baker Book House, 1965. Professor Barnette has an early and extraordinary grasp on how the Orthodox Church so rapidly gravitated away from the New Testament universal priesthood model.

Beckett, John, *Loving Monday*, Downers Grove, IL, Intervarsity Press, 1998. John Beckett is a modern-day Christian businessman who has walked out what he believes to be a call of God on his life to exercise his gifts in the world of commerce. This book describes his search for validation of that.

Butler, Dom Cuthbert, *Western Mysticism*, Dover Publications, Mineola, NY, 2003. Originally written in 1922 by Butler, a Benedictine Abbot; it is a major treatment of the teachings of Augustine, Gregory, and Bernard on Contemplation and the Contemplative Life.

Chesterton, G. K., *Orthodoxy*, Wheaton, IL, Harold Shaw Publishers, 1994. First published in 1908, this book by Chesterton, a former agnostic and academic giant of the twentieth century, formed a theological framework for the likes of Tolkien and Lewis and lays out the simple plausibility of traditional Christianity that still speaks to us today.

Clair, Robin Patric, *Why Work?* 1 West Lafayette, IN, Purdue University Press, 2008. An attempt to describe and define work from a secular perspective.

Coelho, Paulo, *The Alchemist*, San Francisco, Harper Collins, 1993. A fictional best-seller about Santiago's attempt to find his "personal legend," or call in life. Contains many biblical truths.

Forbush, William Byron (ed.), *Fox's Book of Martyrs*, Grand Rapids, MI, Zondervan, 1968. John Fox first published his monumental compilation of the horrors of the church in English in 1564. It was considered so important that many churches of the Reformation chained a copy of it to the pulpit next to the Bible.

Guinness, Os, *The Call*, Nashville, TN, W Publishing Group, 2003. A biblically based, thorough-going study of the claims God makes on our life as a unique individual, leaving no escape for those who demure about having a call of their own.

Hardy, Lee, *The Fabric of This World*, Grand Rapids, MI, Wm. B. Eerdmans Publishing Company,1990. This book is a concise history of thinking that started with Greek Dualism and led up through the Reformation on philosophies affecting our secular work. A very helpful read for me.

Oyer, John S., and Krieder, Robert S., *Mirror of the Martyrs*, Intercourse, PA, Good Books, 1990. A description of the persecution by the orthodox church of Anabaptist believers after the Reformation.

Peabody, Larry, *Secular Work Is Full-Time Service*, Fort Washington, PA, Christian Literature Crusade, 1974. The title says it all. Larry was one of the early pastoral writers on this subject and has worked both in the world of the church and commerce.

Pearcy, Nancy, *Total Truth*, Wheaton, IL, Crossway Books, 2005. A scholarly approach to the Christian's responsibility to know and defend the Christian worldview.

Sayers, Dorothy, *Creed or Chaos*, Manchester, NH, Sophia Institute Press, 1974. This 1949 book states forcefully that it does matter what you believe. For Sayers, doctrineless Christianity is not only impossible but dangerous. She was one of the first moderns to point out that the church must get out of its walls into the workplace and speak into it.

Schaeffer, Francis, *A Christian Manifesto*, Wheaton, IL, Crossway Books, 1982. Dr. Schaeffer shows how the reestablishment of the Judeo/Christian foundation is the only way to turn the tide of moral decadence and loss of freedom in our society.

Smith, Christian, *Going to the Root,* Scottdale, PA, Herald Press, 1992. This is really a plea for reenergizing the church by looking harder at house churches, the role of women, and those of us in the workplace. Professor Smith laments the lack of a workplace theology.

Stevens, R. Paul, *Doing God's Business,* Grand Rapids, MI, Wm. B. Eerdmans Publishing Company, 2006. A comprehensive history of the attitude of the church toward work. It could be used as a textbook.

Tozer, A. W., *The Pursuit of God,* Camp Hill, PA, Christian Publications, 1993. A modern Christian classic on the nature of God for those in the "fellowship of the burning heart," as he put it.

Verduin, Leonard, *The Reformers and Their Stepchildren,* Grand Rapids, 1964, This is a very studied examination of the differences between the Reformers and the Anabaptists. A good reference book on the theology separating these two branches of Protestantism and how they played out in the arena of everyday activities, i.e., work.

Volf, Miroslav, *Work in The Spirit,* Eugene, OR, Wipf and Stock, 1991, To vocation and calling, Volf has added the dimension of cooperating with God by working in the Spirit, leading to a transformation of the world rather than the destruction of it in the end times. It is intriguing as a theology of work, and a twist not seen anywhere else.

Warren, Rick, *The Purpose Driven Life,* Grand Rapids, MI, Zondervan, 2002. More study guide than prose narrative, this book has stimulated many Christians to remember their unique heritage, especially as a gifted child of God, and that we have been created to lead a purposeful life in a way no one else can.

Weber, Max, *The Protestant Ethic and the Spirit of Capitalism,* Mineola, NY, Dover Publications, 2003. This book, first published in the early nineteenth century, has stirred both praise and controversy for its crediting the Protestant movement with a major part of the huge prosperity of Capitalism in the West.

Wilkinson, Bruce, *The Prayer of Jabez,* Colorado Springs, CO, Multnomah Books, 2000. This is an exposition of a simple prayer prayed by the man Jabez in I Chron. 4:10. It has greatly affected the lives of many who have read it, including me.